NUREMBERG

Portrait of a European City

Lorenz Bomhard/Rainer Elpel

NUREMBERG

Portrait of a European City

Disclaimer

All of the information stated in this book has been carefully researched by the author and dilligently fact-checked by the publisher. However, in the legal sense of product liability, content-related errors cannot be completely ruled out. All information is stated without any legal liability or guarantee on the part of the author or the publisher. The author and the publisher rule out any form of liability for content-related discrepancies, as well as for any personal, property or monetary damage.

Bibliographic information published by the Deutsche Nationalbibliothek

The Deutsche Nationalbibliothek lists this publication in the Deutsche Nationalbibliografie; detailed bibliographic data are available in the Internet at http://dnb.d-nb.de <http://dnb.d-nb.de>.

Hans Carl Verlag
© 2006 Fachverlag Hans Carl GmbH, Nürnberg
All rights reserved

Photos: Rainer Elpel with the exception of the following pages: Bernd Telle: page 120; Asmus DIE LUDWIGSEISENBAHN, Copyright (©) 1984 Orell Füssli Verlag AG, Zürich: page 35; Germanisches Nationalmuseum: pages 32, 121; Siemens Corporate Archives: page 125; Stadtarchiv Nürnberg: pages 18, 30, 40, 75; Verlag Nürnberger Presse: Wilhelm Bauer, pages 11, 13; Ray D'Addario, pages 46, 47
Cover design: Publishing service Rohner, Tegernheim
Layout: Publishing service Rohner, Tegernheim
Translation: Wayne Lempke
Photographic reconstruction: Echtzeitmedien, Nürnberg
Printed by Dr. Cantz'sche Druckerei GmbH & Co.KG, Ostfildern

ISBN 978-3-418-00117-3

Contents

Foreword

Nuremberg: That's the view of the city's massive walls with their towers and its fortress built atop a sandstone cliff, with its half-timbered houses and their bull's-eye window panes. In spite of the terrible destruction which took place here in World War II, the city today once again lives up to its mythical status as a medieval gem, which goes back to its rediscovery in 1793 at the beginning of Romantic era. Nuremberg's architecture, with its many gothic buildings, is the result of a rich legacy after a long, successful era which extended into the Renaissance and Reformation. Its grand churches and the city's old town with its narrow streets – this is only half of the story of modern Nuremberg, a city which today is home to half a million people. With the 19th century came Nuremberg's second golden age, thanks to the inventiveness and famed humor of its inhabitants. This period also clearly made its mark on Nuremberg's architectural landscape.

Outside the city walls, Nuremberg is dominated by structures built in the prosperous years of its 19th century industrialisation. This architecture includes elaborate mansions and a local variety of Art Nouveau from around 1900, today known as the Nuremberg Style.

Darker chapters of history also left their mark on the modern city. The Nazi Party took advantage of the glorious medieval backdrop which Nuremberg provided, turning the city into a convention center for its party rallies. The famed architect and Nazi armaments minister Albert Speer designed buildings on a gigantic scale. Nuremberg has confronted its past by placing the so-called *Dokumentationszentrum* (Documentation Center) in the former grounds of the Nazi Party Rallies. As a *City of Human Rights*, Nuremberg has received international acclaim for setting a counterpoint to its Nazi past.

Also part of Nuremberg's legacy is its history as a city of the labor movement, fighting to achieve social justice and affordable housing. This movement was well under way during the Weimar Republic, and regained momentum after 1945. The economic standing of metropolitan Nuremberg continues to grow, positioned in the middle of Europe, just as it was when the historic roadways and trade routes of the Middle Ages met here.

Modern Nuremberg is more than Gothic, more than the city of the Nazi Party Rallies and the racial purity laws which were decreed here, more than its most famous son and artist Dürer and more than just "Führer", more than just *Bratwurst* and ginger bread house romantic. This book proclaims the magic of a city which is nearly one thousand years old, a cultural and historic focal point in Europe.

Lorenz Bomhard

Left: A cozy little spot in the Pegnitz River – view from the Fleischbrücke *(Meat Bridge) of the* Liebesinsel *(Love Island).*

CITY HISTORY

City history

Pages 8-9: City of contrasts – modern buildings offset the architecture of the historic old town. Nuremberg is surrounded by a belt of forests and parks.

RICH HERITAGE

In Nuremberg, a consciousness for history is deeply rooted in its inhabitants. The city's history is considered to be extensively studied, thanks to the work of generations of researchers. The task of discovering the city's history has never been solely left to schools, universities, archives, museums and libraries. Nuremberg's residents have long formed clubs and organizations which actively participate in researching their native city and preserving the rich heritage of their city and its various quarters. Increased interest in city history was gained in the past with special anniversary years and the numerous publications which accompanied these commemorative festivals. 1971 marked the 500th birthday of Albrecht Dürer, 1985 was the 150th anniversary of the railway in Germany, and 2000 marked Nuremberg's 950th birthday. In 2006, the city celebrated its 200th year under Bavarian rule.

History is considered to be an obligation in this city, accompanied by a certain sense of duty to address the dark chapters of Nuremberg's history. As of 2001, the Documentation Center at the Nazi Party Rally Grounds aims to clarify the causes, effects and historical context of the Nazi terror Regime. Since 1995, the former city of the "Racial Purity Laws" has awarded the International Nuremberg Human Rights Award.

Nuremberg's origins

Generations of historians wrote of Nuremberg originating as a "wild root", or a weed. The settlement which would later become Nuremberg did not begin as a Roman outpost, and the mass migration of the peoples toward the end of the Roman Empire also brought only little movement into this region.

The small, meandering, unpredictable river Pegnitz isn't comparable to the navigable waters of the Rhine or Main, and the city's distance to the Baltic, North and Adriatic Seas measures at least 700 kilometers. Mentionable natural resources were also not to be found in the region.

Nevertheless, this "wild root" grew within a few centuries into a large European city. Today the city has, together with its neighboring cities, achieved the status of a major metropolitan area.

A document from the era of emperor Heinrich III, written in Latin and dating from July 16 1050, is the first written piece of history to mention "Norenberc".

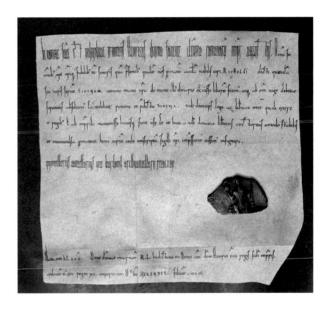

Nuremberg is first mentioned in history in the Sigena document from the year 1050. The document granted the slave freedom from "the burden of bondage".

"In the name of the holy and inseparable trinity. Heinrich, by God's grace, Holy Roman Emperor. A proclamation to all faithful subjects today and for later days. We have set free a slave named Sigena, who having been brought forth to us by the honorable Richolf, having belonged to him, and setting her free by removing a penny out from his hand. We have removed her from the burden of servitude, so that this woman named Sigena may as of now enjoy the same rights and freedoms as those who have likewise been freed by kings and emperors. And such that this freedom presented to her by us be lasting and unchallenged through the power of the law, we have created this document, certifying it with the embossment of our seal.

I, Wintherius, in the name of the Arch-chancellor Bardo, have verified its correctness. Decreed on 16 July in the year 1050 of the year of our Lord, in the third Roman tax year, but in the 21st year of the rule of Lord Heinrich, the third king and the second emperor of this name, in the twelfth year of his royal reign, in the fourth year of his emperorship. Having come to pass in Norenberc. Good luck. Amen."

A legal act with the symbolic gesture of releasing a slave named Sigena marked Nuremberg's entry into the history books, perhaps as a love story: similar sources from the period of Heinrich III come to the conclusion that the nobleman Richolf wanted to either marry his slave Sigena or legitimize his already existing relationship with her. Her emancipation would

City history

Right: "For eternity", as Emperor Sigismund ordered in the year 1423, were the Imperial Insignia to be kept in Nuremberg.

have permitted her to marry while securing the legal status of any children she may have had. Nothing else is known about the destiny of the couple.

The Sigena document, written during Heinrich III's visit to Nuremberg, was merely a peripheral event. The emperor had chosen the area at the foot of today's castle as a strategic point from which he could secure his territorial power. It has been proven that his father, Konrad II, had spent time at the royal residence in "Megelendorf" (today Mögeldorf, now belonging to the city of Nuremberg) in 1025 and again in 1030. The residence in Mögeldorf was located on a bank above a ford in the river Pegnitz, approximately five kilometers east of the 50-meter high sandstone cliff which would later become the fortress hill. According to this information, the decision to use the sandstone hill as an official gathering place must have been made around 1040. In the year 1050, when the Sigena document was written, Heinrich held court at the fortress cliff in Nuremberg to explain the threat which Hungary posed in the southeast of his empire. In 1062, edicts were declared granting Nuremberg market and minting rights and the right to levy tolls, confirming rights which had already been given to the settlement in 1040 by Heinrich III.

First flourishing

Among the early impulses for growth in Nuremberg was the veneration of a hermit named Sebald. The legendary hermit died around 1070 and was buried in Peter's Chapel located at the site which would later become St. Sebaldus Church. Shortly after his death, pilgrims began visiting his grave.

Royal estates which existed in the area before 1050 also attracted settler. Below the fortress hill stood an estate near the Scottish monastery St. Egidien, which dates back to 1140. The Sebald quarter was originally considered to be of higher standing, and housed the old nobility. In addition, it was and is home to the town hall. On the other side of the river in the Lorenz quarter, one of the earliest settlements is thought to be the royal estate near the church of St. Jakob, the place where in 1209 the *Deutsch-*

It is written/ that either emperor Friederich the fourth/ or emperor Ferdinand the first/ or both of them/ (since things can be done by more than one) once asked a councillor/ and, as said Dresserus likes, / Lord Antonium Tucher/ how one could govern such a large group of people?/ Upon which the Lord councillor replied: With good words/ and tough penalties.
Matthäus Merian, 1641

ordenskommende (Commandry of the Order of Teutonic Knights) was founded. This oval-shaped settlement, located on the south side of the Pegnitz, was mentioned in Hohenstaufen documents and dates back to 1150. Still today the surrounding principle streets lead east-west, crossed by small alleys. Here in the Lorenz quarter as well, impulses for economic growth came from trade routes and skilled craftsmanship, leading to the development of a confident, flourishing bourgeoisie.

While the church and the crown were competing for power and influence, Nuremberg was able to flourish in the shadow of this conflict, having been bestowed with the privileges of secular power. A source from 1219 explained that Nuremberg was granted these special rights to compensate for the city's bad location. Very few plants grow on the sandy soils around the city, there were no vineyards here, and the river Pegnitz was unsuitable for shipping.

Originally, two individually-walled settlements developed. Not until 1245 were they considered to be an entity, described historically as a "universitas civium". However, it wasn't until 1323 that they were physically connected by one city wall, incorporating both the Sebald and Lorenz quarters on both sides of the river.

Nuremberg was a favorite child of its rulers and regularly profited from new privileges, not only from trade and toll levying. In his 1356 "Golden Bull" decree, Karl IV ruled that the ceremony of electing the Roman-German kings would take place in Frankfurt, and the coronation in Aachen. In addition, he decreed that each new elected ruler was to hold his imperial diet in Nuremberg.

The significance of Nuremberg being an exclusive member of a trio of imperial cities grew even further in 1423: Emperor Sigismund declared Nuremberg to be "for eternity" the keeper

City history

of the Imperial Regalia. In 1424, under the authorisation of Pope Martin V, the Insignia of the German emperors entered the city, hidden under a shipment of fish from Hungary. They were held in the *Heilig-Geist-Spital* (Hospital of the Holy Spirit). Sigismund had decided on Nuremberg because it was considered to be unconquerable with its massive fortifications.

In exchange for storing and guarding the treasures, the city was annually allowed to put these objects of immense symbolic significance on display, on the second Friday after Good Friday. Following this day, a 14-day trade fair was hosted in the city. The Royal Regalia and Relics fascinated Nuremberg natives and visitors alike. Medieval religiosity led people to believe in the strong healing powers of the objects on display.

The treasure of the Empire

The Imperial Regalia are the only medieval European crown treasures which have survived nearly completely intact. The imperial crown, scepter, sword, and orb are today kept at the Hofburg in Vienna. The Insignia, also known as the "Emperor's Symbols" in the Middle Ages because of their Imperial origins, are a collection of secular objects of symbolic importance, but also of religious relics. The oldest objects date back to the 8th century, for example the Carolingian holy spear, which according to legend contains a nail from Jesus' cross. Slightly younger in age are the Imperial *Evangeliar*, which was kept, together with the Sable of Charlemagne and the *Stephans-bursa*, in Aachen.

Most of the objects of the Regalia were however held for safekeeping in Nuremberg, including a splinter of wood from Jesus' cradle, a tooth of John the Baptist, the relic containing a piece of the tablecloth used during the Last Supper and a piece of cloth which is supposed to have originated from a garment belonging to John the Baptist. All coronation garments also belonged to this collection, including a coat, stockings, shoes and gloves dating back to the 12th and 13th centuries. Only on the occasion of coronations in Aachen, and after 1562, when they were moved to Frankfurt, did the Imperial Regalia leave Nuremberg, under the supervision of a delegation of city councillors.

Johann Wolfgang Goethe jested in 1764 during the coronation of emperor Joseph II in Frankfurt:

"… The young king dragged himself in under the weight of the monstrous pieces of garments, the Insignia of Charlemagne, as if playing dress-up, to such a degree that not even he could keep from laughing. The crown, which would have needed to be fitted, stood away from his head like a hovering roof."

As the French army was approaching Nuremberg in 1796, the Imperial Regalia had to be rushed off into safety. Via Regensburg, the treasures were

This city … is pleased to hold the emperor's regalia, including his vestment. Sword, scepter, the cross-bearing orb and crown of the great emperor Karl which they store in Nuremberg, in order to bestow faith upon the coronation of the Roman Kings through the holiness and old age of those artifacts …
Hartmann Schedel, 1493

brought to Vienna. In the following decades, Nuremberg repeatedly attempted to have the objects returned, but Vienna flatly refused the city's request.

Under completely different circumstances, the treasures returned to Nuremberg in 1938. The Nazis put the Imperial Regalia on display in the "city of the imperial party rallies" in the *Katharinenkirche* (Church of St. Catherine). At the beginning of the war, the Insignia were brought to a bomb-proof bunker built to store works of art (location: *Obere Schmiedsgasse)*. In 1946, the Allied council agreed to have the works returned to Vienna by plane. Since 1954 they have been available for public viewing at the Hofburg in Vienna.

On display at the *Germanisches Nationalmuseum* (Germanic National Museum) in Nuremberg is a copy of a house-shaped silver shrine which contained the relics stored in the *Heilig-Geist-Spital* (Hospital of the Holy Spirit). For security, the shrine was held on a chain and hung so high at the center of the church that it was out of reach for potential thieves.

Nuremberg's glory years

On top of the symbolic value of the Imperial Regalia, real territorial interests came into play. In 1427, at the end of the burgrave era, the city's citizens demonstrated their power and wealth by purchasing the castle and jurisdictional and hunting rights outside of the city. Even more significant was their power struggle to obtain political autonomy from the Burgrave, and later especially from Margrave Albrecht Achilles. To defend itself, Nuremberg built the last ring of walls around its city, a wall which today is still largely intact. This smouldering conflict went on for over 100 years, and when it did actually break out it helped to increase the self-confidence of this economically powerful city-state, a place which magnetically attracted the best artists of the day.

This era is among the greatest in central European urban history, an era which is connected to some of the greatest names of the day, began in the 1420s and extended over a hundred years thereafter. Even today the city

Nuremberg, Latin Norimberga, a large, rich and famed Free Imperial City and a great city of trade, also called the fatherland of cleverness and the home of artists.
Paul Ludolph Berckenmeyer, 1720

profits from its former glory, an era in which it was at the cutting edge of modern times in the arts and sciences, a time when the city took on a central role and its narrow alleyways witnessed a considerable degree of openness for new influences.

PROMINENT NUREMBERG CITIZENS IN THE 15TH AND 16TH CENTURIES

Johannes Regiomontanus (1436-1476) was a Wunderkind of the late middle ages. His real name was Johannes Müller. This astronomer and mathematician later renamed himself after the Latin translation of his hometown, Königsberg in Franconia. Already at the age of eleven he began his studies at the University of Leipzig and calculated the position of all the planets for every day of the year 1448. Later stages of life brought him to Vienna, Rome, Venice and Padua, before coming to Nuremberg in 1471. He settled here in the hopes of finding stimulating academic discourse and hoped that the renowned metal craftsmen of the city in "quasi centrum Europae" would be able to produce the best astronomic instruments.

Regiomontanus was a leader in determining geographical locations on the high seas – his methods were incorporated by Christopher Columbus on his famed voyage in 1492. As a mathematician, he further developed the field of trigonometry. He even tried his hand at astrology, completing a horoscope for Lenore of Portugal, Friedrich III's bride. He was not all that convinced of his efforts: "The stars don't determine, they merely tend toward something". Regiomontanus died in Rome, where he had been summoned by Pope Sixtus IV to work on a calendar reform.

Hartmann Schedel (1440-1514) was a comprehensively educated doctor of medicine, having studied in Leipzig and Padua. Portions of his important book collection are kept today at the Bavarian State Library. From these books, which were partially copied by his own hand, he attained his

City history

In his "World Chronicle" from the year 1493, Schedel included a detailed depiction of Nuremberg with its castle, its churches, its densely built-up the old town and its city fortifications.

knowledge of world history. A retelling of this history named for him was published by Anton Koberger with editions in German as well as in Latin. Schedel's book, richly illustrated at the studio of Michael Wolgemut, documents with his brand of realism the transition from the Middle Ages to the Modern Era.

Schedel, a passionate collector, notated approximately 130 multi-part musical works into one of his notebooks. Today the autograph, known to musicians as the "Munich Songbook", is kept in Munich.

Veit Stoß (before 1450-1533) is one of Nuremberg's great artists. Having grown up in Horb on the Neckar River, he came to Nuremberg in 1473, and was active as a sculptor, wood carver, copper engraver, painter, designer and businessman. In 1477 he gave up his rights as a citizen of Nuremberg to move to Krakow, where he worked until 1489 on the great altar in the *Frauenkirche* (Church of Our Lady). This prominent citizen of Krakow was able to reside there tax-free. His fame grew continually. King Kasimir IV Jagiello commissioned Stoß to build his grave of red marble in the Vavel Cathedral. Bishops followed the king's example and also had Stoß work for them.

In 1496, Stoß returned to the city on the Pegnitz River and renewed his Nuremberg citizenship. The reason for his return was probably the poor health of his wife Barbara, who was originally from Nuremberg. She died in the same year.

The first piece from this creative period dates to 1499: the Volkamer Epitaph in the East Choir of St. Sebald Church. This is comprised of three sandstone reliefs with scenes from the Passion of Christ. The following years were marked by legal battles between the artist and the council. Stoß had allegedly counterfeited promissory notes in retaliation for being cheated on in a textiles deal. The crime brought him in 1503 the public branding of "dishonest man": with fire-hot iron, both cheeks were branded. The artist then fled to the parish church in Münnerstadt, where he encased an altar by Tilmann Riemenschneider. In 1506 he was pardoned by the emperor.

He received commissions from the wealthy Tucher family. For Endres Tucher he carved a very large figure of the Apostle Andreas, which today stands in St. Sebald Church. Anton Tucher commissioned the Angel's Greeting, a depiction of the annunciation in the rosary, which hangs in the upper choir of St. Lorenz Church. Further works by Veit Stoß include the crucifixes in St. Lorenz and in St. Sebald, as well as the Bamberg Altar, which was commissioned by the artist's son, the prior of the Nuremberg Carmelites, and today stands in the southern nave aisle in the Bamberg Cathedral. The carving illustrates the birth of Christ. Prior Andreas is depicted in the carving as a shepherd wearing the traditional clothing of his order.

City history

Adam Kraft (ca. 1455/1460-1509) left behind an impressive body of work in a short period of time. From 1490 until his death, this sculptor and architect completed numerous commissions, for example the Schreyer-Landauer Epitaph on St. Sebald Church and the House of Sacraments in St. Lorenz, on the bottom of which he also incorporated a self-portrait. The relief designed for the municipal weighmaster's building as well as the seven stations of the way of the cross and his crucifixion ensemble are today kept at the Germanic National Museum. As an architect, Kraft worked on the gable of the choir of Michael at the *Frauenkirche* (Church of Our Lady). His special talent was bringing his figures and artistic scenes to life.

Martin Behaim (1459-1507) followed in the footsteps of the astronomer Regiomontanus. Originally he was sent by his uncle, the councilman Leonhard Behaim, to Flanders to learn to become a textile tradesman. Barely 20 years old, he opened his own business and travelled to the island of Fayal in the Azores. There he made contacts with the Portuguese royal family, and at the age of 25 was called into the service of the *Junta dos matematicos*. He was charged with making advancements in nautical sciences. He was familiar with Regiomontanus' discoveries and was able to locate his geographical position on the high seas, for example while on an expedition to southwest Africa. When Behaim returned to Nuremberg in 1491 for a few years, he was working on a plan to place the known continents of the earth on a globe – before the discovery of America. In 1493 the project was completed with the help of the graphic artist **Georg Glockendon** (around 1450-1514), who painted the globe, and Hartmann Schedel, the author of *World Chronicle*. A map of the world by Behaim is no longer in existence.

The cosmographer died a poor and lonely man at the German Bartholomew Hospital in Lisbon, after falling out of favor with the Portuguese court for getting involved with matters of throne succession.

Peter Vischer the elder (1460-1529), with his most significant work, the St. Sebald shrine, represents the transition from the Gothic to Renaissance era. His father Hermann had been the proprietor of a renowned foundry whose works included a baptismal font for the church in Wittenberg (1457). His son, Peter, made the chandelier for St. Lorenz Church (1489), and successively received the commission to create the grave for St. Sebaldus. His first design from 1488 was a late gothic, approximately 12 meter-high artwork. The shrine which he ended up building in 1519 is exactly 4.71 meters tall and combines style elements of the Gothic era with figure ornamentation more typical of the Renaissance. Both Vischer sons, Hermann and Peter, were involved in creating the shrine, having been stylistically influenced by travels to Italy.

Caritas Pirckheimer (1467-1532), was born Barbara Pirckheimer, and received the name Caritas at the age of 16 when she became a nun of the Poor Clares Convent. Conrad Celtis, with whom she exchanged letters, wrote her a poem:

"Virgin, most beautiful creation on German soil, Caritas, in my heart the most dear, most divine virgin."

From 1503 until her death, Caritas Pirckheimer was the abbess of the St. Clara convent. As a highly-educated woman, she was an important contact in the city. After the Reformation she remained, in spite of attacks on her convent, faithful to her old beliefs. She held long conversations with Philipp Melanchton. In her work *Denkwürdigkeiten* (things worth noting), the abbess describes the years of the Reformation. She was buried "at the first grave at the chapel door near the votive basin". The gravesite was forgotten and wasn't re-discovered until 1959. It is located in the Church of St. Clara.

Willibald Pirckheimer (1470-1530) was a scholar, translator and publisher, respected throughout Europe. His thorough knowledge of ancient Greek was widely famed. Correspondence and encounters with leading intellectuals were also numerous: Thomas Morus dedicated the Swiss edition of his work *Utopia* to the humanist Pirckheimer, who was in intense discourse with Erasmus von Rotterdam.

Since his youth, Pirckheimer had been a friend of Albrecht Dürer's, who, being a member of the Inner Council, did his utmost to sponsor him. His relationship to the Reformation remained ambiguous. First a supporter, he later became a critic of the movement, also because the Council had caused his sister's convent so much grief. He eventually believed that the Reformation, because of its uncompromising nature, endangered the purpose of humanism and even the Empire.

Pirckheimer, who had achieved the position of Imperial Councillor, was unafraid of expressing unpopular opinions. The scholar also thought geopolitically: After America and the ocean route to East India had been discovered, he was concerned about the future of the metropolis of trade which Nuremberg had become. He feared that overseas trade could lessen the significance of the city in the middle of Europe – in favor of the Netherlands, but especially Spain and Portugal. As an example he continually spoke of Venice's loss of power.

Albrecht Dürer (1471-1528) is Nuremberg's most famous son. His family background demonstrates how Nuremberg magnetically attracted gifted craftsmen to the city: Dürer's father was originally from Hungary, having come to the Pegnitz River as an apprentice goldsmith. Three years before the birth of his famous son, he attained the city's rights of citizenship. His last name was also given to him by the city: Albrecht the elder had been born in the city of Ajtós (Eytas) in Hungary. "Ajtó" means "door" (German "Tür"), which became "Türer", pronounced "Dürer" in the local Franconian dialect.

The goldsmith was frequented by prominent customers, including emperor Friedrich II and Cardinal Albrecht of Brandenburg. According to tradition, his son was also to become a goldsmith. But the junior Albrecht discontinued his apprenticeship. He instead went to the painter Michael

Right: "Der Hase – Hommage á Dürer", is the title the artist Jürgen Goertz chose for his bronze hare which faces Dürer's home on Tiergärtnertor.

Wolgemut to receive his training. Like his father, he went on an apprentice's journey, travelling to the Netherlands, then up the Rhine to Basel. Upon his return to Nuremberg in 1494, he was quickly married to Agnes Frey. His father and the respected metal craftsman Hans Frey had arranged the marriage. The 23 year old Dürer seems not to have taken the marriage all too seriously. Just a few months after the wedding he packed his bags and left for Venice. His trips to Italy – a second was undertaken from 1505-1507 – shaped the artist. He came back with new ideas and expanded his repertoire beyond religious themes:

"Real art is to be found in nature - he who can tear it out has it."

He studied the human body exactingly, he carefully painted a hare, grass – his works leave out no natural detail.

His fame is owed nevertheless to a religious work: in 1498, St. John's revelations inspired a wood carving. His godfather, Anton Koberger, printed the "Apocalypse", and later the Passion Cycle. Soon Dürer's book of commissions was full. In 1509 he purchased the home known today as the Albrecht Dürer House (located at *Tiergärtnertorplatz*).

Dürer's legacy isn't just about the works of a painter, drawer and chiseller. He authored books on measurement, printmaking and the principles of proportion. His planned work, "The Great

City history

Shoemaker and poet: With a shoemaker's apron and a book in his hand, this monument dating to 1873/1874 honors the poet Hans Sachs, located at the square named for him near the Heilig-Geist-Spital.

Book of the Art of Painting", remained uncompleted, just brief essays on art theory came to print. Books, letters and diaries display his remarkable linguistic talent, also through regular and extensive correspondence with the greatest minds of his era. From his vast body of work, relatively few have survived, including nearly 90 paintings as well as approximately 1,000 copper engravings, wooden carvings and book illustrations.

Hans Sachs (1494-1576) was already a legend in his own day: 6,000 poems recorded in 33 hand-written books were left to us by the "old German poet". According to the perceptions of the 18th and 19th centuries, his image falsely stood for a stuffy, bourgeois lifestyle and for amateurish poetry. New admiration for his work was won through the romantic glorification of Nuremberg. His most prominent advocate, more than 200 years after Sachs' death, was Johann Wolfgang Goethe.

National glory for the "Old German Meister" came for Hans Sachs thanks to the new opera by Richard Wagner, "Die Meistersinger von Nürnberg", which saw its world premier in Munich in 1868. Within a few years, the opera was standard repertoire in every major city. The composer Wagner, who liked to sign with the name Hans Sachs, followed the tradition of the "German Meister" with his singspiel, which was praised in its day for its patriotism. His own hymn of praise is sung by Hans Sachs in the finale "Honor your German Masters, to conjure up good spirits!".

Who was Hans Sachs really? Poet, master singer, a disciple of Martin Luther's, an author of critical texts on the peasants' and the margrave wars. As a shoemaker, he became wealthy, but he owed his fame to his prolific production of religious and secular texts. In 1523, two years before the Reformation in Nuremberg, he authored the pamphlet "The Nightingale of Wittenberg". This work was preceded by an unusual three-year creative hiatus. His complete works cover nearly 70 years. Later, his pro-Reformation essays were widely published. Within this time he exercised critique of old religious beliefs only sparingly. His writings focused on the theological content of the Reformation and encouraged "God-pleasing considerateness".

POPULATION

Statistics clearly show what an attractive city Nuremberg had become: cities with more than 10,000 inhabitants were regarded in the middle ages and early modern age as major cities. Among the cities which had a population of over 20,000 in the early to mid 15th century were Ulm, Lübeck, Gdansk and Hamburg.

Among the largest German cities were Cologne, Augsburg and Nuremberg, seeing their populations around 1530 increasing to over 40,000. For Nuremberg, this was a 100 percent increase in population in just 100 years. Exact censuses weren't recorded however until the beginning of the 19th century. Some estimate that Nuremberg around the turn of the 16th century was home to around 50,000 people. Accounts of rising grain consumption and a shortage of living quarters are among the contemporary sources which support this estimate.

The plague, smallpox and dysentery – just within a few years, the population of the city was decimated by various epidemics. Only through high birth rates and continuous migration could the population loss be offset. Some epidemics led to the loss of a quarter of the population within just a few months, as did the plague of 1562.

Between the prime years of the free imperial city until the annexation of Nuremberg into Bavaria in 1806, the population of the 1.6 square kilometer old town had decreased to 25,000.

Nuremberg's revival around the time of its industrial revolution helped the city to grow rapidly. Also contributing to this development was the annexation of the neighborhoods outside the city walls in 1825, when Gostenhof, Wöhrd, today's Nordstadt and St. Johannis, Galgenhof and portions of today's Südstadt were incorporated into city territory. This created plenty of space for modern production. By 1850 the city had grown to 50,000, and by 1881 to over 100,000. At the turn of the 20th century, the city numbered 260,000, and another 100,000 were added by the beginning of World War I in 1914.

The annexation of further outlying areas in the late 19th century didn't increase the population much further. 35,000 people were added in 1899 by the annexation of 13 outlying suburbs, but they increased the size of Nuremberg from 1300 hectares to 5500 hectares. The neighborhoods of Schniegling, Thon, Wetzendorf, Schoppershof, Erlenstegen, Mögeldorf, Gibitzenhof, Schweinau, as well as Muggenhof located along the railway to Fürth were all added to Nuremberg. Within a few years, these new neighborhoods had been filled with thousands of new residents.

This extreme growth in population however didn't only bring immense economic growth, it also came with immeasurable social anguish. The last quarter of the 19th century, a period of enormous economic success, was also a period of disappointment and loss: of the 450,000 who came to the city during that period, 350,000 would eventually leave.

From 1918 till 1939 the city's area continued to grow through annexations. Building construction was strong and housing developers had their hands full. From a population of 360,000 in 1914, the city grew to 420,000 at the beginning of the war in 1939.

According to statistics, only 178,000 still dwelled in Nuremberg in the spring of 1945; the number conceals forced laborers and prisoners of war. Nearly 300,000 were registered in the city already by spring 1946, just a year after the end of the war.

Reconstruction, a large amount of housing development and especially the annexation of further areas – Großgründlach, Neunhof, Katzwang, Worzeldorf, Kornburg, Fischbach, Brunn and vacant land previously belonging to the village of Schwaig allowed Nuremberg after 1972 to grow to a city of over half a million. Its population has stabilized to around this number ever since.

Nuremberg's area has also increased immensely: when it became part of Bavaria in 1806, it joined with its medieval format of 1.6 square kilometers, but by 1899 had expanded to include 54,5 square kilometers of land, and by the year 2000 to over 190 square kilometers.

City history

The artful Sebald Chörlein, *or little choir, was attached to its mother-house in 1370. The original, which was made of sandstone, can be viewed at the Germanic National Museum. A granite reproduction today adorns the building.*

FROM THE REFORMATION TO THE END OF THE FREE IMPERIAL CITY

Among the privileges which Nuremberg enjoyed, including keeping the imperial regalia and hosting post-coronation imperial diets, a further status symbol was granted the city in 1500: the Imperial Regiment. The Estates of the Empire and emperor Maximilian I agreed to form this 20-member committee to serve as an acting governing board. Nuremberg seemed to be an ideal meeting place. The city hall provided board members protection from the sometimes conflicting interests of power between the emperor and prince-electors. However, differences with the emperor and the troubles which Nuremberg had with the Margraves of Ansbach led to a quick dissolving of the committee, after only two short years' time.

Upon the formation of the second Imperial Regiment of 1522-1524, the Estates of the Empire and emperor Karl V again agreed on Nuremberg as a meeting place. However, the Imperial City's reformational zeal displeased Archduke Ferdinand. For this reason the Imperial Regiment was moved to Esslingen, which was at the time still true to the "old faith".

The era of the Reformation is generally considered to be a time of downfall in the Imperial City. Although Nuremberg's status was no longer that which it was in Dürer's era, trade and craftsmanship, the arts and sciences continued to flourish in the tradition of the city's earlier generations.

Characteristic *Chörlein*

Attesting to the continuing wealth and unwavering interest in design in the period after the reformation are the *Chörlein* (little choirs), or alcove additions to residences. These richly elaborate additions to facades were for centuries a characteristic of Nuremberg's architecture. These little choirs originally served as in-home altars. Gothic, Renaissance, Baroque and especially the Rococo era: each period created its own *Chörlein*, made of stone or wood – even into the 19th and 20th centuries, attempts were made to keep up this tradition. Until the end of World War II, 400 such additions graced the city's facades, not including the smaller window-choirs which had come out of fashion and had been nearly completely removed. Thanks to the initiatives of an organization known as the *Altstadt-freunde* – friends of the old town – and its long-term president **Erich Mulzer** (1929-2005), about a fifth of all pre-war *Chörlein* have been rebuilt and are again part of Nuremberg's townscape.

The high price of emperor-cult and the end of city council rule
Nuremberg's emperor-cult was an expensive life insurance policy for the city. The city, located in the middle of the Franconian Imperial Circle, expected protection by the emperor from its combative neighbors, especially from the margraves of Brandenburg-Ansbach. Nuremberg had an ongoing feud with Ansbach. More than 300 expensive court proceedings were carried out between the factions before the imperial councillor. Military conflicts also burdened the city financially, including the second war with the Margraves (1552-1555), which brought severe devastation to Nuremberg's outlying areas.

The Thirty Years' War brought further destruction and great economic strife to the city in the years 1632-1635. In 1632, Gustav II Adolf and Wallenstein took part in a positional war with each other right at the gates of Nuremberg. By intervening, the Swedish King Gustav Adolf prevented the re-catholicisation of Nuremberg. He futilely attempted to stop the imperial army from joining forces with the Bavarian military. Initially the Swedes built a wide wall of defence with entrenchments around Nuremberg (an example for this is the *Bärenschanze,* or bear's trench). Wallenstein's troops held camp in Zirndorf. The battle between the two forces at the *Alte Veste* (Old Fortress) in Fürth brought great losses to both sides. Without a victor, both sides withdrew. More than 60 percent of the population lost

City history

their lives in the chaos of the war, in a city overflowing with refugees. On top of all of the battling, a 1634 outbreak of the plague cost 20,000 lives. The city's vast debts had to be paid off by its wealthiest families.

After the Peace of Westphalia of 1648, Nuremberg hosted in 1649 a subsequent convention and a peace banquet, which marked the final end to a long war.

Soon the emperor was back asking the city for more money. The war against the Turks and the War of Spanish Succession devoured millions of

July 4, 1650: Fireworks at the shooting ranges in St. Johannis, commemorating the peace banquet of 1649.

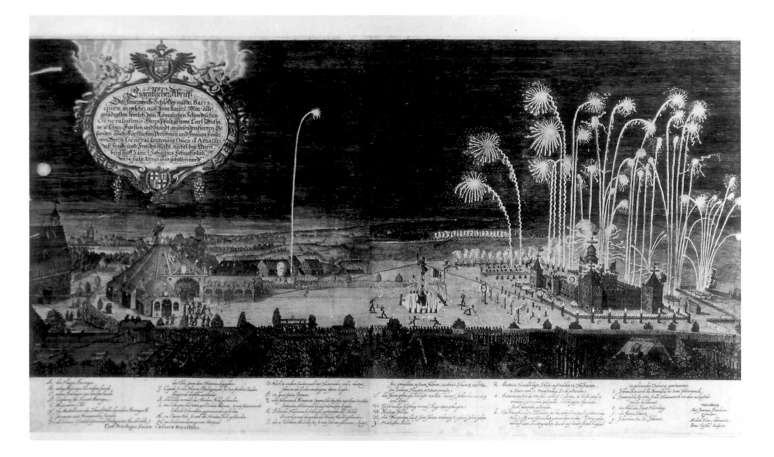

guilders – Nuremberg sacrificed itself for the emperor and the Empire, ruining itself in the process. In 1712, the last emperor, Karl VI, entered the city to much pomp, decorated by garlands and an arch of triumph. The city's devotion to the Empire took on grotesque characteristics: Protestant Nuremberg helped to finance the Seven Years' War against Protestant Prussia.

The city continued to increase its debt by borrowing money from its wealthy citizens. However, the patrician council still refused to give its wealthy donors a say and even refused to open their books to them. Some began protesting when the council raised taxes or levied special fees, and opposition started to organize in the 18th century. Not until 1792 were merchants allowed to have a say in the finance commission of the grand council.

1794 saw the end of sole patrician rule in Nuremberg: a new committee consisting of 70 patricians, 70 prominent businessman, 70 craftsmen, 20 civil servants and 20 scholars was now to lead the city. The new constitution between the patrician council and the new members didn't hold up long and led to new conflicts. In 1797, a special delegation sent by the emperor stripped the commission of its powers and appointed a new board which was made up of 24 aristocratic and eight untitled senators, who stayed in power until 1806.

In velvet and silk

The dress code of the Nuremberg council from 1693 makes clear distinctions in the city's social classes – and clearly demonstrates the competition between the new rich and the old aristocrats in power. The dress code was an attempt to maintain the status quo in class distinction and to make it more evident as to who belonged to which class. Six classes are listed in the dress code. In great detail it was listed who was allowed to wear velvet, silk and damask, woven fabric or leather. The upper class – the members of the old, established, aristocratic patrician families – was naturally allowed to wear the finest dress. The second tier consisted of merchants who were also

The patrician dynasties, 26 families altogether, whose members form the council, have many advantages over *Patriciis* in other Imperial Cities. First, they enjoy sole authority and control over the city, which in the *Interregno* of most other Imperial Cities has to be shared with its citizenry. They have always kept their nobility pure, for none of their ranks have married below their class, so that no-one but they may enter into the council, save for those whose impurity goes back four generations. They can attest to their good breeding, not as in other Imperial Cities having mixed with commoners. They equal the real nobility in all respects, apart from living in the city and mixing more and more with common folk, which was at one time considered to be quite usual and harmless.
Johann Brandmüller, 1742/1744

SPONSA PATRICIA
Normbergenſis.

members of the grand council; they weren't allowed to wear velvet. The third group, which consisted of merchants and prominent craftsmen, were only allowed to wear lower-quality silk. Belonging to the fourth group were small businessmen and craftsmen. Grocers and low-ranking craftsmen made up the fifth group. At the bottom of society were maids, servants and apprentices.

Reserved for nobility were buttons made of metal: such a detail was also strictly regulated. By the 18th century, craftsmen and merchants also began wearing metal buttons. There was not only a dress code for men, detailed regulations were also dedicated to women's attire. The council also stipulated which luxuries were allowed at family weddings and baptisms. There were many contradictions in the code, especially as consciousness for fashion and high-quality materials and jewelry increased among the upwardly mobile middle class.

Romantic discovery

An excursion from Erlangen to Nuremberg made by two students would later go down in cultural history: in 1793, the Berlin natives **Wilhelm Heinrich**

Wackenroder (1773-1798) and **Ludwig Tieck** (1773-1853) meandered down the narrow streets of the old Imperial City. The two 20 year-olds were less interested in the reasons for political and economic decay taking place in this city, where many of its rich traditions dated back to the middle ages. They projected their glorified view through the passionate perspectives of the Storm and Stress period in literature, in search of the likes of Albrecht Dürer and Hans Sachs in this ancient city. Nuremberg was a different type of city: there was little space and money here for baroque architecture. There had been scepticism toward new trends after the French Revolution, preferring to get back to the roots of medieval and early modern times.

With the literary glorification of his time spent in Nuremberg, Wackenroder provided the impetus for a whole movement of adoration for Nuremberg by later generations: "The outpouring of the heart by an art-loving friar" was the subtitle of his work which recounted his "romantic" feelings for the city which had fallen upon him. Meanwhile, Wackenroder's writings marked the beginning of an era which would be known to following generations as the Romantic era. All the great writers of the day began coming to Nuremberg: Joseph von Eichendorff, Achim von Arnim, Clemens Brentano and E. T. A. Hoffmann. One side-effect of this movement was the fact that painters and even some Nuremberg natives intensively began to deal with preserving the historic images of the city and the heritage of this former focal point of Europe.

In this manner, a Nuremberg school of painting emerged, whose works depicted the narrow streets and Gothic buildings in romantic lighting. A monument worthy of a king was built in Albrecht Dürer's honor: the bronze statue north of St. Sebaldus Church by Jakob Daniel Burgschmiet towers 2.5 meters high, supported by a 3.5 meter sandstone base. The original plans for this work of art date back to 1826, in preparation for the elaborate celebrations in 1828 commemorating the 300th anniversary of the artist's death. The statue was dedicated on Dürer's birthday, on May 21, 1840.

Left: Colored copper plates from the 19th century tell of the dress code decreed by the council in 1693. The image shows a patrician bride in an elaborate dress, valuable jewelry and an artful bonnet.

... The men of the first or patrician estate may attach fir to bonnets made of velvet; the women and maids of the old noble families and of the foremost estate may wear bonnets of velvet but not all too large, rimmed with fir, which they may only wear on high feasts decorated with golden roses or beads but not with diamonds. Completely golden hair bonnets may not be decorated with beads. Women are warned to refrain from wearing collars of disproportionate length or thickness, as well as cloaks, especially those adorned with expensive lace, because this is considered highly immoderate.
Dress code of the Nuremberg city council, 1693

City history

Wurm's forced administration

Nuremberg's success in the 19th century had an unpleasant beginning: **Christian Wurm** (1771-1835) was the name of the man who until 1818 nearly single-handedly attempted to solve the city's problems after it was annexed into Bavaria. These issues had previously been the responsibility of the imperial ruling class.

The turn of the 19th century was accompanied by huge deficits in the city treasury. Wurm had previously worked for the royal Prussian authority in Ansbach and in Fürth. He lost his job due to overreaching and his harsh style of governing. But when the Bavarians took over Nuremberg, they were grateful to be served by this merciless lawyer, hoping to incorporate this former imperial city into centralized Bavaria. Wurm soon made many enemies among the city's inhabitants, who had traded in patrician oligarchy for the sole authority of a Bavarian civil servant. Because of the enormous debts which Nuremberg had amassed, the bronze latticework of the town hall's main hall was dismounted and sold in 1806. Suffering similar fate was the Shrine of the Deocarus Altar, which was melted down in 1811. Wurm had grand plans for the city and wanted to raze the city walls, giving it a modern appearance. His tenure also witnessed the reorganisation of the municipal public order office, the building authority, the construction of schools and the ban on manure heaps in the city.

Ambitious plans

As soon as King Max I Joseph had conceded more local power to cities in 1818, Nuremberg grew increasingly ambitious. Two men played a pivotal role in bringing the industrial age to their city. **Jakob Friedrich Binder** (1787-1856) was elected Nuremberg's mayor for life, and **Johannes Scharrer** (1785-1844) was elected vice mayor. Schools, flood protection, bridge renovation, the founding of a municipal savings and loan, street lighting fuelled by canola oil and later by gas, the founding of a polytechnic school where **Georg Simon Ohm** (1789-1854) began teaching in 1833 – in the beginning decades of the 19th century, Nuremberg was a city of pioneer advancements.

It comes then as no surprise that plans to build the first German railroad, which first travelled from Nuremberg to Fürth in 1835, were forged here. This spurt of innovation brought long-term success to Nuremberg's compa-

The first German railway on its maiden voyage from Nuremberg to Fürth: frightened onlookers and horses shy away from the monstrosity. This portrait dates to 1935.

nies which manufactured for the railroad. **Theodor von Cramer-Klett** (1817-1884) modernized his father-in-law's factory, bringing it into the industrial age. Out of this company, 14 years after his death, the engineering works of Augsburg-Nuremberg were formed, today better known as MAN. The mechanical engineer **Ludwig Späth** (1786-1854), along with Cramer-Klett, are among the top-ranking industrialists of the age.

Gingerbread and telephones

This dynamic age was brought upon with the efforts of several great entrepreneurs and industrialists. The ultramarine manufacturer **Johannes Zeltner** (1805-1882) had been a trader of hops; the pencil manufacturer **Johann Lothar von Faber** (1817-1896) was also one of the charter members of a life insurance company, founded in 1884; the gingerbread maker **Heinrich Haeberlein** (1820-1867) developed a system for the mass production of *Lebkuchen*; **Julius Tafel** (1827-1893) founded a steel-mill in St. Jobst.

Heinrich Berolzheimer (1836-1906), a native of Fürth, had been a successful pencil manufacturer in the United States. After his return, he was an active philanthropist in Nuremberg and Fürth.

A good example of the innovative abilities of Nuremberg's natives is **Friedrich Heller** (1836-1911), who began producing electric doorbells in 1860, and introduced one of his own inventions, the intercom, in 1877, bringing telephones into several homes and offices.

Sigmund Schuckert (1846-1895) was among the leading pioneers of 19th century Germany: he set new standards in electrical engineering.

Kaspar Hauser

Swaggering, wearing tattered clothing and shoes, a boy named Kaspar Hauser (ca. 1812-1833) arrived in Nuremberg on the afternoon of May 26, 1828, the Monday after Pentecost, a day which would later go down in history. He was holding a letter addressed to a "high lord cavalier, member of the 4th Esgatoron of the 6th Scholisch Regiment in Nierberg". The letter stated that the boy, now approximately 14 years old, as an infant had been

What a place of enlightenment Nuremberg was! This single city has done more for innovation, art and science than entire nations.
Friedrich Campe, 1828

laid at the doorstep of day laborers. He had never been allowed out of the house, but was well-mannered. Influential citizens supported the boy financially, and he became somewhat of an exotic attraction. Wild speculation still surrounds his supposed aristocratic origins, for a time some even suspected Napoleon of having fathered him. Attempts to uncover his identity have been made by DNA analysis of blood traces found on clothing which is still in existence, but nothing has shed light on the mystery of his origins.

Kaspar Hauser himself provided no clues in solving the puzzle of his identity. He monotonously repeated that he wanted to become a cavalier like his father. When interest in his story began to wane, he attracted attention by injuring himself in 1829. Four years later, according to legend, an unknown assailant stabbed him in a park in Ansbach. However, it may have also been a last, desperate attempt by the 21-year-old Hauser to attract attention to himself. In any case, the repercussions in the literary world were extraordinary. This foundling soon became one of Nuremberg's most famous sons.

Exorbitant rents and outbreaks of tuberculosis

The downsides of Nuremberg's industrial revolution, accompanied by a population explosion, hit the poor the hardest: living quarters were scarce, often resulting in exorbitant rents. Tuberculosis thrived in overcrowded housing. Social upward mobility was hardly possible. Until laborers were given the right to marry in 1868, it was only possible through high bureaucratic hurdles to receive permission to marry and have a family. The result: about a third of all children born in a given year were illegitimate. The workers' discontent led to a labor movement, which gained momentum in the late 19th century. In 1848, a year of revolution and economic crisis, protestors in Nuremberg held the "enemy" in Munich responsible for their strife. Separatism, in this case independence from Bavaria, was propagated.

On the municipal level, the years of extreme economic and population growth in the last quarter of the 19th century were marked by massive development projects: paved streets, a sewage system, gas (later electric)

Criminals to be punished outside of public view were subjected to the dungeon's iron maiden. As soon as the executioner, according to a chronicle, touched its pedal, its blades cut the criminals into little pieces, which fell right into the sewage beneath. This method is called "sending the poor sinners to the fish". The construction and implementation of the iron maiden dates back to 1533. *Johann Ferdinand Roth, 1812*

city lighting, a central slaughterhouse, a supply of drinking water – Nuremberg had to be brought up to modern urban standards within just a few years. Impressive buildings from the turn of the century display the wealth of the era. 36 new schools, all of which are grand buildings, were built by the city in the boom years between 1870 and 1914. Also from this era are the hospital in the north of the city, the artists' house at Königstor and the *Gewerbemuseum* (Industrial Arts Museum) located at *Marientorgraben*. The first world war brought this second coming of Nuremberg to a bitter end.

Years of famine in the Great War

Within just a few weeks after the war had broken out in 1914, misery was on the rise. The export-oriented economy was brought to a standstill for a lack of customers. There were hardly any workers left for production anyway, since most had been drafted into the military. The city was forced to provide free meals on a grand scale. The conversion of the metal works to arms manufacturing plants in the second year of the war brought some relief to the city's families. However, looting in grocery stores was still a daily occurrence.

DURING THE WEIMAR REPUBLIC

A difficult new beginning

Nuremberg enjoyed a peaceful order of events during the November Revolution of 1918. Its inhabitants were war-weary. Images of the misery suffered at this time have survived: young soldiers who had lost arms and legs on the killing fields, hungering children, ailing elderly. Nuremberg lost 9,855 soldiers in the war. In the first years after the war had ended, thousands fell victim to epidemics which plagued the city, including influenza and tuberculosis.

A basic problem had been postponed between 1914 and 1918: there was still a housing shortage. Construction projects were undertaken by workers' and soldiers' organizations, and later the municipal authority with public housing projects, creating jobs and living space for families. The history of Loher Moos and Buchenbühl in the north of Nuremberg are textbook examples of housing issues during the Weimar Republic. A group of men returning from the war occupied a section of forest, which in 1922 was still outside city territory, clearing the wood. The state was unable to put a stop to it. Later, the occupation of the land in Buchenbühl was legalized with certain criteria, stipulating that gardens and small farm animals must be maintained and kept on the land. In the beginning, mainly laborers and craftsmen dwelled in the "red settlements". A few years later, homesteads were added in Loher Moos, many of which were purchased by civil servants. The progressive city government even located an artists' colony there, providing special lighting conditions for art studios. In the Nazi era, new housing policies placed Nazi Party members in the settlements.

The era of Luppe

The 1920 election of **Hermann Luppe** (1874-1945) to the office of mayor was a very fortunate event for the city. He had worked as an attorney for the city of Frankfurt/Main and had become acquainted with all of the dealings of municipal business. As one of the founders of the Weimar constitutional party, the German Democratic Party, he announced his candidacy, allying himself in Nuremberg with democratic leaders, relying on the principles of social democracy. Luppe only had a few years to shape modern Nuremberg in spite of many hurdles: first inflation, then high unemployment resulting from the economic crisis of 1929, then Nazi raids on the city and finally the Nazi takeover.

With the help of city planner **Hermann Jansen** (1869-1945), Luppe had bold visions for the city, including the plan to put an expressway on the bed of the former *Ludwigskanal* (Ludwig Canal) – later to become the *Frankenschnellweg* (Franconian Expressway). Around the city walls, a ring road

City history

was to be constructed. One of his planned projects never took off: Nuremberg and its neighbor city Fürth were to merge into one city.

Luppe, a native of Kiel, and Jansen of Berlin had underestimated local sensitivities on this issue.

A chapter of the city's history is connected to Luppe's name, an era which would serve as a role model after the second world war: exemplary housing projects, social and health care policy, as well as the construction of recreation and athletic facilities and liberal cultural policies.

1928 marked the climax of the policies of the era: there were festivals marking the 400th anniversary of Dürer's death, the dedication of **Otto Ernst Schweizer's** (1890-1965) planned stadium and adjacent private gardens, "athletic facilities for everybody", a stadium pool and restaurants.

An attractive athletic facility was long overdue in the city: Nuremberg led nation-wide in such disciplines as weight lifting and wrestling, bike racing (Nuremberg was a center of bicycle manufacturing), motor sports, but especially revered in soccer. The First Football Club of Nuremberg won the title of German master five times between 1920 and 1927.

... In secret I was expecting all sorts of wonders in this Gothic city ... but none of that was to be found. The city made a terrible impression on me, which naturally was not the city's fault, but mine alone. I saw a truly enchanting old town ... I saw St. Lorenz and St. Sebald, saw the city hall with the court where the fountain stands so ineffably charming. I saw it all,

and all of it was beautiful, but it was all surrounded by a large, unloving, barren business town, filled with the noise of rattling engines, strangled by automobiles, everything quietly shook to the tempo of a different age unfamiliar with reticulated vaulting, not knowing how to install fountains as fair as flowers in quiet courtyards, everything seemed about to collapse within the next hour, for it had no longer any purpose or soul.

Hermann Hesse, 1925

DARK TIMES

Julius Streicher (1885-1946) founded a Nuremberg chapter of the Nazi Party in October 1922 and had become a fierce opponent of the mayor, Luppe. Violent conflicts broke out between Nazis and democratic forces in 1923, killing one worker – the beginning of a number of brawls between the Nazis and their political opponents in Nuremberg. Shortly thereafter, Streicher and his Nazi Party received 11 percent of the vote in municipal elections, gaining seats on the city council. With primitive antics – including slander and harassment – Streicher attempted to defame the ruling mayor. Nobody was able to put a stop to him, he even had supporters among the state police.

In 1923 he began circulating an anti-Semitic inflammatory pamphlet, *Der Stürmer,* earning him applause from party leaders. On March 9, 1933, the Nazi Party seized control of Nuremberg's city hall. They had never earned a majority of seats in the city, but the NSDAP simply transferred national election results to the local level and overthrew city leaders. Mayor Luppe was even put in jail. He died in 1945 during the last days of the war in his home town of Kiel.

By 1933, Streicher had achieved his goal. When the Social Democrats refused to support him in the city council, he had them beaten up by thugs and had them deported to the concentration camp in Dachau. One of his victims was the working-class poet **Karl Bröger** (1886-1944). Under Streicher's rule, Jews were publicly persecuted already in 1933, bringing on an exodus of Jewish citizens from the city. The list of criminal activities committed by Streicher and his supporters is endless. In the meantime, he and his party filled their own coffers, attracting the attention of Nazi Party leaders. Streicher was thrown out of office in 1940 for not transferring enough of the looted monies to the central treasury. Already weeks before the famous pogrom on the night of November 9, 1938, which was especially brutal in Nuremberg, Streicher had publicly called for the demolition of the main synagogue on Hans Sachs Square.

At the same time, Nuremberg was also a city of resistance. **Joseph E. Drexel** (1896-1976), who in 1945 began his tenure as publisher of the leading local newspaper *Nürnberger Nachrichten,* was among the most tenacious of regime opponents. Various groups of Social Democrats and Communists attempted to smuggle in flyers from abroad. In St. Lorenz, pastor **Wilhelm Geyer** (1892-1978) courageously spoke of "sin and injustice" after the night of pogroms in 1938.

City of the party rallies and racial purity laws
Adolf Hitler loved Nuremberg. In 1927 and 1929, he chose Nuremberg's historic center as the backdrop for his party conventions. From 1933-1938, around one million people convened annually in the "party rally city". Leni Riefenstahl's famous 1934 propaganda film "Triumph of the Will" brought the images of the party rallies to millions more. Quasi-religious rituals were invented by party masterminds for the occasion. Allegiance sworn to Hitler, the "Messiah", was a fixed ritual in the program, as well as military exercises played down as "battle games". In 1934, the architect and later armaments minister **Albert Speer** (1905-1981) was put in charge of designing a "sacred site of the [Nazi] movement": a gigantic area for military parades, including a "German Stadium" with a capacity of 400,000; the *Zeppelinfeld* (Zeppelin Field) with a seating capacity of 70,000; the *Kongresshalle* (Congress Hall) and the *Große Straße* (Grand Way) for parades. The only

facility completed by the time the war broke out in 1939 was Zeppelin Field.

What Streicher had long been writing in his inflammatory pamphlets became official party policy in 1935, when the Nazis proclaimed the racial purity laws, preparing the way for the holocaust. With the passing of a new "civil code", Jewish citizens were stripped of their civil rights. The "law protecting German blood and German honor" forbade all romantic relationships and marriages between "Arians" and Jews.

Half-finished ruins bear witness to the colossal scale of Albert Speer's architecture. After taking over the city, the American Army detonated the giant swastika. The stone grandstands at the former Reichsparteitagsgelände (Nazi Party Rally Grounds) are today a popular venue for recreational activities, and accommodate spectators during auto races.

The perfidy of National Socialist philosophy was evident in the motto of the convention which was planned for September 2, 1939: The so-called "Peace Rallies" didn't take place, since the Wehrmacht had just marched into Poland days before.

Demise under the hail of bombs

The beginning of the war turned Nuremberg, a city of metal production, into a capital of arms production. Vehicles, engines, detonators and grenades were made here. While the men were off to battle, the women had to take over in the factories. Soon they were assisted by forced laborers from the occupied territories, estimated to have numbered around 100,000. In the meantime, Jews were being deported out of Nuremberg into concentration camps.

Schöner Brunnen, the famed beautiful fountain located on the *Hauptmarkt* (Main Market Square), had been covered under a protective coat of concrete, while precious artworks were moved into bunkers after war had broken out in the city in the fall of 1940. Bombs also fell on the *Reichsparteitagsgelände* (Nazi Party Rally Grounds). On August 29, 1942, the first of a series of heavy bombing impacted the old town, culminating in the hail of bombs which hit the city on January 2, 1945. On this one night alone, one million firebombs and 6,000 explosive bombs fell on the city. All told, during 59 various bombardments on the city, 3 million firebombs, 60,000 phosphorous canisters and 32,000 explosive bombs were dropped. More than 8,000 people lost their lives in these air raids, and approximately 13,000 were injured. Of the 372,000 people living in the city in 1942, only 200,000 remained by the end of the war.

By April 1945, when American ground forces entered and took control of the city, all that was left of this once glorious Gothic town was debris, ruins and more than ten million cubic meters of rubble. 95 per cent of the original structures in the old town were destroyed. On April 20, 1945 – Hitler's 56th birthday – the American Army held a victory parade on the Main Market Square.

Page 46 and 47: After being heavily hit by bombs during World War II, Nuremberg was mostly rubble and ashes. Only five percent of the buildings in the old town survived the war unscathed. Photographs from 1945 show the view of the castle from the Main Market Square with its destroyed Frauenkirche *(Church of Our Lady, page 46) and the Albrecht Dürer monument surrounded by rubble (page 47).*

JEWS IN NUREMBERG

The history of the Jews in Nuremberg up to 1945 is a particularly horrible chapter, ranging from exclusion, expulsion and execution. Their presence in Nuremberg is first historically recorded in the early 12th century, when Jews turned former swampland east of today's Main Market Square into habitable ground. In 1298, 628 Jews were murdered. The excuse given was alleged desecration of communion wafers. Among the victims was one of the most renowned Talmudic scholars of the middle ages, Mordechai ben Hillil.

The main synagogue built in 1874 (domed construction, back right) was a dominating feature of Nuremberg's skyline. In August 1938, its demolition was ordered by Julius Streicher. A commemorative plaque located at the site tells of this sacrilege.

City history

But then such a fate in the last lost decades: Streicher and Hitler, the "City of the party rallies", and the city of the "Nuremberg Laws" and then as a contrast the city of the "Nuremberg Trials" – shall the name of the venerable Noris be smeared by history and remain tainted! The wonderful glory of its past, its self-portrayal as an urban and sophisticated, a humanistic and humane spirit, was defenceless to that which happened next to it and within it.
Theodor Heuss, 1952

Murder and confiscation marked the pogroms of 1349 as well, when the city of Nuremberg seized the Jewish quarter. Then in 1499, with the emperor's permission, Jews were driven from the city "for good". For 350 years, there was no Jewish community in Nuremberg. Not until 1850 was a Jew, Joseph Kohn from Markt Erlbach, granted permission to reside in the city, a procedure accompanied by lots of bureaucratic red tape.

Nuremberg's Israeli Cultural Community was founded in 1862. The synagogue which was burned down by the Nazis in 1938 had been built on Hans Sachs Square in 1874, while another synagogue was built on Essenwein Street in 1902. Jewish citizens played a pivotal role in the city's economic and cultural development. 42 Jewish charities and foundations have been recorded in the city. Patriotically-minded, 1,550 Jews from Nuremberg went to fight as soldiers for Germany in World War I. Already by the 1920s, they were subjected to evil hate crimes instigated by Julius Streicher and his thugs. The Jewish community numbered 10,000 around that time, shrinking to just 50 in 1945.

It is impossible to put a number on the barbarism of the Nazis. Expulsion, escape, deportation to concentration camps, brutal attacks often ending fatally, theft and state-sanctioned confiscation: approximately a fourth of all members of Nuremberg's Jewish community were killed during the Nazi regime. In spite of this bitter history, Nuremberg Jews re-established a new Israeli Cultural Community, and later built a synagogue. Nuremberg's post-war Jewish history is strongly connected to Arno Hamburger, who was a long-serving city council member and head of the Jewish community, a man who built inroads to new understanding.

THE NUREMBERG TRIALS

Just a few months after the end of the war, Nuremberg was back into spotlight: The Palace of Justice, constructed form 1909-1916 in a neo-Renaissance style, had survived all of the bombing nearly unscathed and was put into use by the American military. Also because of its adjacent jail cells, it seemed to be an ideal location for an international military tribunal. In Courtroom 600, leading prosecutor Robert H. Jackson opened hearings, at which 24 prominent Nazis were placed on trial, including Hermann Göring, Albert Speer, Rudolf Heß and Julius Streicher, the former Nuremberg mayor. In October 1946, the court handed down the following verdicts: twelve of the accused were sentenced to death by hanging, including Streicher. Hermann Göring poisoned himself with cyanide just hours before his execution. Twelve further proceedings took place in Courtroom 600 till 1949.

The Nuremberg Trials were a first step in detailing the atrocities committed by the Nazis, making them known to the world. More than 400 international journalists came to report on the trials, including the authors Alfred Döblin, Ilja Ehrenburg, Erich Kästner, Susanne von Paczensky and Gregor von Rezzori. The later chief of the East German intelligence service, Markus Wolf, the futurologist Robert Jungk and later West German Chancellor, Willy Brandt, were among those to report on the events.

THE NEW NUREMBERG

The plan was obvious: the ruins of the old town would be removed by bulldozers, clearing the way for a new Nuremberg. But local citizens wanted to avoid what was being done in most other German cities after World War II following the immense devestation.

Already during the war, **Heinz Schmeißner** (1905-1997), who would later become Nuremberg's long-serving city engineer, was working on plans to rebuild. The view from the castle over the old town reveals his concept: the original contours of the buildings were to remain intact while keeping the steep medieval roof lines, thereby restoring the city's original visual charac-

City history

Right: The Dokumentationszentrum *(Documentation Center) at the former Nazi Party Rally Grounds distances itself architecturally from the unfinished* Kongresshalle *(Congress Hall). Like a foreign body, the new research facilities clearly hover over Albert Speer's original building.*

ter. Those witnessing the rebuilding of all these historic homes and churches were astounded by the activity.

Because of the proximity to the Iron Curtain, Nuremberg had been robbed of its central position in Europe until 1989. Nevertheless, Nuremberg was successful in rebuilding its economy. Large companies like AEG, Diehl, Grundig, Siemens, Quelle and Photo Porst, on top of many other firms, brought years of economic growth to the city. Some economic sectors like the metal and electronics branches didn't fare so well and were faced with mergers and plant closings. The service sector grew in importance, with firms such as the *Gesellschaft für Konsumforschung* (Consumer Research Company) and DATEV, which provides software systems for accountants tax advisors.

From 1957 till 1987, mayor **Andreas Urschlechter** (born in 1919, first serving as a Social Democrat, later as an independent) determined the city's fortunes. With further annexations of outlying areas and the new urban planning in Langwasser, Nuremberg grew to a population of half a million.

The city received recognition in 1995, exactly 60 years after the passage of the racial purity laws, for introducing the Nuremberg International Human Rights Award, which ever since has been awarded every other year.

The first prize money was donated by **Hermann Kesten** (1900-1996). This Jewish author with Nuremberg roots had been forced to emigrate in 1933. The Israeli artist **Dani Karavan** (born in 1930) designed the *Straße der Menschenrechte* (Way of Human Rights), located at the Germanic National Museum.

A counterpoint to the city's history during the Nazi regime is provided by the Documentation Center, built in 2001 and located in the former Nazi Party Rally Grounds. It is open for exhibitions, lectures and is a center of research.

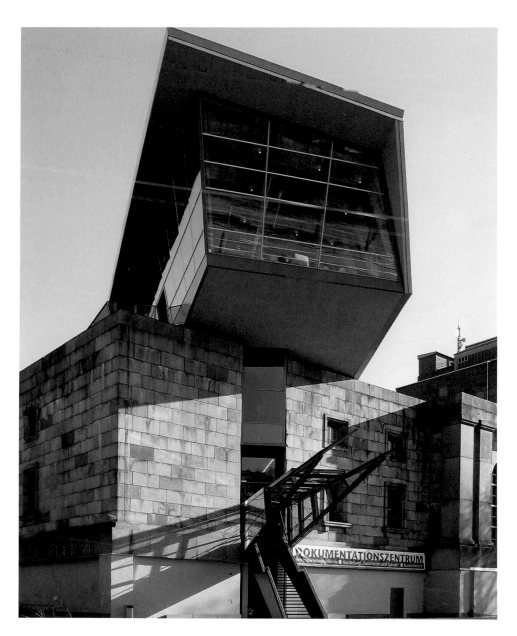

Page 52 left: The Chapel of Walpurgis located in a fortified tower belongs to the former fortress of the burgraves and dates back to the Romanesque period. After being destroyed in the war, it wasn't rebuilt until 1969.

Page 52 upper right: Statues of the twelve apostles adorn the dome of St. Elisabeth. 16 marble columns support the stately dome.

Page 52 lower right: The ponds of the Tucher Brewing Company in the north of Nuremberg used to provide ice for chilling beer. The ice was cut in winter and brought into the cellars for storage.

Page 53 upper left: The Main Market Square is the focal point of the city and a popular venue for various occasions such as this football fan event.

Page 53 lower left: The pedestrian zone and the shops on Karolinenstraße – Nuremberg is a popular shopping destination.

Page 53 right: The Straße der Menschenrechte (Way of Human Rights), designed by Dani Karavan, sets an architectural contrast to the city's role during the years of Nazi dictatorship.

City history

THE CASTLE

The castle

Pages 54-55: View of the castle. At the left the Palas *with the* Heidenturm *(Tower of the Heathens); next to it the* Sinwellturm *(Sinwell Tower), round tower and keep of the* Kaiserburg *(Imperial Castle), to the right the* Kaiserstallung *(Imperial Stables).*

Glorious/ and praiseworthy is the emperor's Palace above the city/ in which the portraits of Roman emperors/ who held court here/ in the great hall/ and in other chambers/ many admirable objects to see/ and what is more/ out of all windows/ not only the city/ with all of its buildings and possessions/ one can view/ but also the whole horizon/ and contours of the countryside/ for taking in a quite beautiful perspective/ of which something comparable will hardly be found in the whole empire.
Josephus Rosazer, Cosmographia

The fortress is unsightly, rambling, old. The old emperors who once resided here must have been very austere. Today any average citizen would have better rooms.
Anselmus Rabiosus, 1796

Right: For centuries, a huge moat protected the castle and the city from enemy attacks. Nuremberg had one of the safest defence systems in all of Europe.

Medieval rulers were also nomads of a sort: they moved with their entourage from one palace to the next, securing their power by showing presence. The modern term "capital" is therefore not really applicable to the practices of the day. But Nuremberg can still allow itself the title of unofficial capital of the middle ages and of the early modern age – thanks to its castle. On more than 300 occasions beginning in 1050, when the city was first mentioned historically, and ending in the late 16th century, German rulers came to the fortress to convene and hold court.

Emperor Karl IV had a special connection to the city: more than 50 visits to the city have been documented. The Golden Seal of 1356 declared that each newly elected ruler was to convene his first diet in Nuremberg. The last Imperial Diet was held in Nuremberg in 1543. Afterwards, the fortress remained under imperial authority, but was frequented very rarely by its owners. Along with the city, the castle came under Bavarian control in 1806. The bombs which fell on the city in 1945 brought great destruction. Only ten years later did reconstruction of the castle begin.

The 200-meter long fortress has been Nuremberg's main landmark for centuries. The *Kaiserstallung* (Imperial Stables) has been converted into a youth hostel, and the museum at the castle is administrated as a branch of the Germanic National Museum.

The castle grounds comprise an area of 10,000 square meters, located on two red sandstone cliffs. The grounds developed architecturally and historically in three stages: portions of the Burgrave castle near the pentagonal tower, the oldest surviving structure in Nuremberg; the *Kaiserburg* (Imperial Castle) built around the central court, and later more buildings dating back to Nuremberg's times as a Free Imperial City.

The oldest portion of the grounds dating back to the 11th century were possibly built on the foundations of an older fortification which may have existed before the year 1000. The good strategic location of the cliff suggests early fortification.

The castle which we see today is the result of continual modifications, expansions and demolition throughout the past centuries. Archeological

digs have uncovered evidence of a residential tower in the center of the Imperial Castle courtyard, probably dating back to before 1100.

In the eastern portion of the rocky terrain, a fortress was built in the 11th century around a keep, the pentagonal tower. This enclosure was the seat of the burgraves – including the Count of Raabs after 1105, and from

Page 58: View from the south of half-timbered facades and castle roofs. In the foreground the Himmelsstallung *(Heaven's Stables), in back the building which houses the* Tiefer Brunnen *(Deep Well).*

57

The castle

1192 till 1427 was administered by the Hohenzoller dynasty. The city's history thereafter was characterized by the desperate attempts by its citizens to remain independent from the influence of the burgraves and later from the neighboring margraves in Ansbach and Bayreuth. The so-called *Luginsland* (as in "look into the land"), built in the year 1377 with four oriels, should have been named "Lug-in-die-Burg" (look into the castle): The city council had it built to keep an eye on the detested burgraves. In 1427 the city purchased the burned-down castle of the burgraves after it had been destroyed during ongoing battles in 1420. The city used the Imperial Stables as a municipal granary, built in 1495 on top of the ruins of the original burgrave castle.

In 1340, Konrad III ordered the construction of a new castle in the western portion of the rocky terrain. This castle, the Imperial Castle was later extended by his successors. Under the reign of emperor Friedrich Barbarossa, the castle became the official emperor's palace or *Palatium*. A wall and the *Sinwellturm* (Sinwell Tower), the only medieval round tower in the city, separated the emperor's palace from the castle of the burgraves. Between the two is a clearing which would achieve special significance under medieval asylum laws. The castle as we see it today dates back to the 15th century. The Imperial Castle received further additions in the late Gothic era – the knights' hall and the emperor's grand hall. Of the original structures, only the double-story chapel remains. Another important monument from this early period is the *Tiefer Brunnen*, a deep well which cuts 50 meters deep through the underlying sandstone.

The youngest portion of the fortress complex is comprised of the imperial city's fortifications toward the west, which were built in the 16th century as part of the municipal defence wall. The plans for the bastions were devised by the Italian fortifications architect Antoni Fazuni.

Above: The Neutor *(New Gate) with its tower was once one of the city's main points of entry. A trade route leading to Würzburg and to Frankfurt/Main began here.*

Pages 60-61: Dense urbanisation and green, open spaces in direct proximity – the castle rises high from behind the fields of Knoblauchsland *(Garlic Country).*

CITY OF CHURCHES

The churches are large, dark masses, full of
art and Gothic embellishments, ornate turrets,
large portals with sculptures etc. There are
many of their kind here ...
Wilhelm Heinrich Wackenroder, 1793

City of churches

Pages 62-63: *The late Gothic* Frauen-kirche *(Church of Our Lady) on the Main Market Square is the oldest hall church in Franconia. Its construction, decreed by emperor Karl IV, was carried out between 1352 and 1361.*

Church history

When Nuremberg entered the history books in the year 1050 by being mentioned in the Sigena document, the church had long since staked out the area. Most portions of what would later become part of the city belonged to the Diocese in Bamberg, while a smaller portion belonged to the Eichstätt bishopric. More than 900 years later, in 1976, the diocese of both cities agreed to grant Nuremberg a main church which would co-operate across diocese borders. But the borders are still largely the same as they were a thousand years ago: the territory of the Bishop of Eichstätt is in the south of Nuremberg, while Bamberg's Archbishop controls the northern section of the city.

Nuremberg's Christian lifestyle was from its very beginnings influenced by an obstructionist: Sebald, who would later become the city's patron saint, was according to legend responsible for numerous miracles. The hermit lived in the first half of the 11th century. He was a member of the reform movement around the turn of the millennium, a movement which protested the amalgamation of church and state, rejecting the conventions of religion and feudal structures. Sebald was buried in St. Peter's Chapel, a small church which once stood on the site of the present Church of St. Sebald. The legends surrounding the hermit soon attracted pilgrims to his grave, bringing money to the young economy of the little settlement beneath the castle hill. Not until 1425 was Sebald – or *Sebaldus* in Latin – canonized by the Vatican.

The church of St. Sebald today is known for its efforts to establish cooperation between Catholics and Protestants looking for common ground between their faiths. The annual St. Sebald day on August 19 is marked by an ecumenical celebration.

The Reformation was a defining moment in church history, a movement which dates back to March 1525 in Nuremberg. The decision of the council members to affiliate themselves with the new teachings had however by this time had a long history. The city had continuously tried to release itself from the confines of church law and from the Bishop of Bamberg. Nuremberg already had been granted a large say in nearly all church affairs, including administration and appointing priests. Already by 1524, priests were holding mass in German. The Reformation was a further step in granting the city power over the church. The city council had already increased its authority regulating doctors, pharmacies and midwives. The city government also concerned itself with social matters such as helping the impoverished. The Reformation movement naturally wasn't only about power and influence: other reasons were a critical attitude toward Biblical interpretation, protesting the unabashed secular lifestyles which members of the clergy had been leading, and finally the outburst of fury over indulgences being paid to the church in return for the forgiveness of sins.

In spite of the long years of conflict during the Reformation, Nuremberg quickly became a center of Lutheranism in Franconia. Even after the Peace of Augsburg of 1555, the Imperial City maintained its religious independence.

As an outward gesture of the Reformation, a school was founded in 1526 with the help of Philipp Melanchton, who had been one of Martin Luther's closest allies since 1519. The Melanchton Gymnasium, a school which today is still in existence, is considered to be the oldest facility of its kind in Germany. Its most famous headmaster was the philosopher Georg Wilhelm Friedrich Hegel, who served from 1808 until 1816, when he was appointed to a professorship at the University of Heidelberg.

The Order of Teutonic Knights remained an enclave of Catholicism after the Reformation. It was founded in Nuremberg in 1209 in the western part of the Lorenz old town. It supervised the famous Elisabeth Hospital, and after 1234 the *Siechkobel*, a home for lepers in St. Johannis. After the Reformation, the Order was forced to relinquish the church of St. Jacob to the city, and only Protestant services were held there after 1532. Prior to this a wooden, covered bridge had been built there leading worshipers to the church without actually having to touch imperial soil. Later, Catholic masses were only allowed to be held in the hospital chapel, at the site of today's St. Elisabeth Church. A small state within the city state emerged,

The beautifully painted stained glass windows in all of these churches are full of magic and emit a warm, sacred gloaming. The display of colors, when the sun shines through, is indescribable: the entire sacred history seems to come to life and move ...
Friedrich Heinrich von der Hagen, 1818

City of churches

Saints Sebald and Laurentius were and are the patron saints of Nuremberg. Sebald is said to have converted heathens here, having come to Germany with Bonifacius under the name of Ewald; according to other sources he was a native German hermit, Säwald, a garlic farmer from Nuremberg. According to legend, a farmer had called him in the night to help find his lost oxen, and Sebald made the farmer's 10 fingers light up like 10 lanterns. And since there was no fire to warm himself, he removed from the roof – shingles? – no! the first icicles he saw and made from them the most wonderful fire – thereafter he was a saint *comme il faut!*
Karl Julius Weber, 1826

surrounded by thick walls. Some fugitive criminals sought asylum within the Catholic compound.

Only 1,100 Catholics were living in the city in 1806 when it became part of Bavaria, a little over four percent of the 25,000 inhabitants which the city then numbered.100 years later, at the beginning of the 20th century, their proportional numbers greatly increased in the wave of industrialisation: with 100,000 members, the Catholic community comprised a third of the population. Two thirds Protestant, one third Catholic – this relation has remained stable up to the present day.

At the beginning of the 20th century, both religious groups experienced a revival. Within the various church congregations, workers' and social clubs were organized, especially in the new neigborhoods in the outlying areas. There was an awakening of spiritual life, as well as church-supported youth and social work beginning in 1902 with the efforts of widely-renowned Protestant theologians such as **Christian Geyer** (1862-1929) and **Wilhelm Stählin** (1883-1975).

Like the rest of the city, the three main churches – St. Sebald, St. Lorenz and the *Frauenkirche* (Church of Our Lady) – were heavily damaged by bombs during World War II. The complex undertaking of rebuilding the Gothic temples was viewed by Nuremberg's post-war citizens as a symbol of survival and as a new beginning in Nuremberg after the horrors of Nazi dictatorship and the war.

Also in honor of the early ecumenical efforts of the theologian Stählin, both religious groups had for decades felt obliged to focus on the common objectives of the Christian churches. They made a special effort to establish intense contact with the Israeli Cultural Community in Nuremberg. Another fixed element of religious life in Nuremberg is the dialogue with members of the Muslim faith.

St. Sebald

According to legend, the people of Nuremberg built the chapel of St. Peter at the exact location where, in 1070 at the foot of the castle hill, a cart pulled by oxen came to a halt. On the cart was Sebald's body. Because of the early onset of the Sebald-cult after his death and the subsequent pilgrimages made in his honor, the hermit's name soon replaced the original name of the chapel. Official recognition from the church first came in 1425 when he was declared a saint. A document from 1386 carrying the seal of Pope Urban VI states that the chapel of St. Peter/St. Sebald had originally been established through the Church of St. Peter in Poppenreuth (Fürth).

Today's church was constructed in four phases from around 1230/1240 until around 1500. The nave and transept, leading back to the west choir, date back to the original late Romanesque construction, a columned basilica from around 1235. In

View from the Schürstab House on Albrecht Dürer Square overlooking St. Sebald and the church's parsonage with its characteristic Chörlein.

1309, the nave aisles were widened and re-designed in the Gothic style. The elaborate construction, worthy of a bishop but in this case merely a city church, attests to the ambition of this emerging city: the double-choired church houses a transept which after 1374 opened to an imposing nave, as well as a crypt with an outside entrance at the west choir with its double-towered façade, an east choir with an apse, crypt and a balcony (known as the *Engelschor,* the Angel's Choir) opening to the center nave. The Gothic remodelling after 1309 brought bigger windows to the west choir, and four elaborate portals which give the church its modern-day appearance. After 1481, the height of the towers was increased. Today their peaks tower

City of churches

77 meters above the St. Sebald old town. Between them, a crucifix from 1625 made by the brass-founder Johann Wurzelbauer adorns the middle window of the west portal. The Schreyer-Landauer Epitaph (1490-1492) by Adam Kraft, along with the church's portals, is among the most impressive works of art on the exterior of the church. The interior of the church is like a treasure vault, bearing witness to the former wealth of Nuremberg's citizenry.

St. Sebald's grave. This work of art originating from Peter Vischer's studio contains the silver-coated reliquary casket.

Four dolphins and twelve snails adorn the base of St. Sebaldus' grave, on which a 4.71 meter-high brass canopy rests. The tomb had been in the works since 1488, but wasn't completed until 1519. It originated from the studio of Peter Vischer the elder. Its reliefs depict the saint's miracles, such as making an icicle burn or restoring vision to the blind. The inclusion of the four classical heroes Simson, Hercules, Nimrod and Perseus, and the depiction of the cardinal virtues as well as cherubs making music and playing attest to humanistic and Renaissance influences, connecting modern Christianity to antique traditions. Self-confidently, the artist also depicted himself: with a hammer and chisel, he stands in the east corner of the grave. On columns overlooking the grave, he placed twelve watchful apostles on pedestals, positioned above them are the twelve prophets of the Old Testament.

Placed at the center of the work is the silver-plated oak coffin. This Gothic relic shrine from 1391-1397, incorporating the municipal and the imperial coats of arms, originated from the workshop of the goldsmith Fritz Habelzheimer.

The ambry (ca. 1370) located in the ambulatory of the church's east choir takes on the appearance of a church façade. This work depicting Christ's tomb attests to the growing veneration beginning in the 13th century of the body of the son of God.

Stained glass paintings were commissioned by patrician families already in the 14th century. Three of the windows date back to the 16th century. According to drawings made by Albrecht Dürer, Veit Hirsvogel is thought to be the artist responsible for the 1514 depiction of emperor Maximilian, who also commissioned the window portraying various rulers and coats of arms of the lands under Habsburg rule. The margrave window, donated in 1515 by Margrave Friedrich von Brandenburg-Ansbach, depicts his family and its Hohenzoller domain, implicitly reminding viewers of the old territorial claims of the burgraves. The Bishop of Bamberg also commissioned a window in 1501 according to plans by Albrecht Dürer: 24 years after this demonstration of power, the council decided to follow Luther's teachings instead.

A playful cherub on the grave of Sebaldus; this photograph shows the artful details of the work's figures.

City of churches

The rose window and the twin spires on
the western façade of St. Lorenz above
the portal of sculptures.

Lavish altars bear witness to the generosity of the patricians: the Haller Altar (ca. 1440), the Altar of St. Catherine (ca. 1462-1464), commissioned by Wilhelm Löffelholz, and the Topler Altar (1477), donated by Nikolaus Topler. This work by Veit Stoß is adorned with several treasures, including the three stone reliefs and two oak figures of the Volkamer Memorial Endowment (1499); the Tucher family donated a basswood sculpture of the Apostle Andreas (ca. 1505); the figures of the crucifixion group (1507/1508 and 1520) located above the table altar in the east choir were completed by Veit Stoß.

Among the church's most impressive art works is the Cross of Nails from the war-ravaged English city of Coventry: it symbolises conciliation between the British and the Germans after the devastation of World War II.

St. Lorenz

The church of St. Lorenz is the younger of the two city parishes. While St. Sebald served as the church of wealthy patricians, St. Lorenz was the people's church: in the southern, newer part of Nuremberg, craftsmen and merchants were the first to settle here, while the patricians' families arrived somewhat later. A triple-nave, Romanesque columned basilica mentioned in a 1235 document was one of the predecessors to the church we see today. The chapel dedicated to St. Lorenz and the Holy Tomb was subordinate to the main parish of St. Michael in Fürth, ruled by the Bishop of Bamberg. The church's Gothic construction was built sometime between 1243 and 1315 – its exact period of construction is not known. The first construction phase was comprised of a Gothic, triple-nave basilica, which made use of stones from the torn down chapel of St. Lorenz. The imposing western façade, with its rose window and its portal of sculptures, can be dated more exactly to the year 1353.

By 1390, construction was completed, and already patrician families started adding their own chapels onto the church. In doing so, the walls of the nave were removed, up to the outer edge of the buttress. The huge orifices which were created were well suited to the installation of glass

The first hours of the afternoon ... I took advantage of them to take a stroll through the city. I first entered the Church of St. Sebaldus, where a baptism was taking place, and I was allowed to enter, although I am not so fond of lingering there, since the most treasured art work there, the grave of St. Sebald, leaves me quite cold. From there however I continued on to the Church of St. Lorenz, where my entire soul was joyful at the sight of these tall, magnificent halls, these gigantic bunches of pillars, these elegantly-formed arches, this sacred semidarkness and the stained glasswork. How one can completely forget any thoughts of Gothic over-embellishment upon seeing such a church!
August von Platen, 1821

City of churches

St. Anne's Altar by Hans Suess von Kulmbach. This work of art can be viewed in the northern ambulatory of St. Lorenz Church.

windows. Continuous alterations to the church during various construction phases also saw the addition of balconies over the side portals.

Between 1439 and 1477, the hall of the presbytery and its ambulatory were enlarged. The builders of St. Lorenz were motivated by competition with St. Sebaldus: the veneration of the city's patron saint in the church at the foot of the castle was to be offset by their own cult honouring Deocarus. In 1316, Ludwig the Bavarian had bestowed the city with relics in gratitude for having supplied weapons. The remains of the abbot Deocarus, Charlemagne's father confessor, were placed in a silver reliquary casket at one of St. Lorenz's altars.

During the course of the following centuries, little changed in St. Lorenz. Patrician reverence for their ancestors and a general consciousness for history saved the church from the mass removal of art during the Reformation which occurred elsewhere. Not until the end of the city's imperial era, when it was taken over by Bavaria, was art irretrievably lost. To help pay off its municipal debts, Deocarus' shrine was melted down for its silver. Copper from a medieval baptismal font and also from gutters on the church's roof were also removed for their monetary value. Within a short time, the church began deteriorating. The damaged interior tracery cross of the rose window was removed. The valuable *Engelsgruß* (Angel's Greeting), created by Veit Stoß in 1517/1518, was removed by Bavarian authorities, placing it in the Royal Gallery in the castle. Later, when it was taken back to the church, the carving crashed to the floor. Years later it was restored. The remains of Abbot Deocarus have been kept in Eichstätt since 1846.

In 1903, an organisation was founded to refurbish the church, and ever since it has seen continuous restoration.

The worst damage was done to the church by bombs during World War II. The ambry had been completely covered by a concrete case. All works of art, including the stained glass windows, had been moved to bomb-proof bunkers, located for example under the castle hill. The Gothic church was hit repeatedly and was transformed into a ruin: in August 1943, on January 2, 1945 when Nuremberg took its biggest hit, and once more at the end of the war, damaged by artillery firing. Only the outer walls and the church's towers stood above the mountains of debris in May 1945.

Nuremberg's citizens donated generously to rebuild the church. However, the largest donation came from New York: Rush Kress, heir of the Kress von Kressenstein family, provided huge sums of money to rebuild the church. On August 10, 1952, on the feast day of St. Laurentius, protestant Nuremberg dedicated its rebuilt nave, celebrating by holding its first post-war service in the church.

The *Engelsgruß* by Veit Stoß and the nearly 20 meter high *Sakraments-haus* (ambry) by Adam Kraft are among the church's most significant art treasures. Chiselled out of light grey sandstone, the ambry depicts passion scenes – according to the wishes of the benefactor Hans Imhoff.

The wealth of the Church of St. Lorenz is evidenced by the detailed work of its 13 main altars. The Krell Altar (ca. 1483) shows in the background of its center section the oldest surviving depiction of Nuremberg. As in St. Sebald, Nuremberg's wealthy families generously contributed to St. Lorenz's art. The ornate windows – for example the Volkamer window and the Haller window, both dating to the year 1480, as well as the Rieter window

City of churches

from 1481 – as well as the memorial plaques bearing various families' coats of arms demonstrate this spirit of philanthropy.

Frauenkirche

The *Frauenkirche* (Church of Our Lady) was built in Nuremberg's late Gothic era. Franconia's oldest hall church was built between 1352 and 1361 at the behest of emperor Karl IV. The square-shaped nave is comprised of two equally high flanking aisles.

The church's architect was Peter Parler (1330-1399), who had worked on the cathedral in Prague under Karl IV. With the coats of arms of the seven prince-electors placed on the balustrade and the portrait of the emperor which was later added, Nuremberg's significance as a Free Imperial City was evoked. Also the *Männleinlaufen* (Running of the little men) – the elaborate clock which dates back to 1509 – on the west façade facing the Central Market Square typifies Nuremberg's special status, laid down by Karl IV in his Golden Seal of 1356. Every newly-elected ruler was to hold his first imperial diet in Nuremberg. At 12 o'clock noon, the seven prince electors dressed in red appear. The seven are the Archbishops of Mainz, Cologne and Trier, the King of Bohemia,

Left: The Frauenkirche *(Church of Our Lady) on the Main Market Square with its characteristic gable, designed by Adam Kraft in 1508.*

Right: The Männleinlaufen *(a special clock) of the* Frauenkirche *(Church of Our Lady) at the Main Market Square is one of Nuremberg's tourist attractions: every day at noon sharp the figures created by Sebastian Lindenast begin turning.*

the Duke of Saxony, the Margrave of Brandenburg and the Palsgrave of the Rhein – they all circle the emperor three times. The church's steep gable was built in 1508, designed by Adam Kraft. A gold and a blue sphere indicate the phases of the moon. Another work by the famous sculptor is an epitaph made for the Peringsdörffer (or Pergenstorffer) family, adorned by a Madonna figure (ca. 1498). This sandstone work of art had been, up to its demolition in 1816, displayed in the Augustinian Church.

The Church of Our Lady has served as the city's Catholic parish church since 1816. The painted plaques hung on the church's pillars date to the 15th century and were salvaged from the Church of the Dominicans before it was demolished. They depict the resurrection of Christ and St. Michael killing dragons. The Tucher Altar (ca. 1445) was originally kept in the Church of St. Veit which was razed in 1816. It is a fine example of Nuremberg painting before Albrecht Dürer.

The fortified Church of St. Georg in Kraftshof

To the northwest of Nuremberg lies the unpretentious fortified Church of St. Georg. The fortress/church is popular among Nuremberg couples seeking a romantic setting for their weddings. Walking through a gate, visitors to the church enter a courtyard surrounded by walls with crenels and peaked fortified towers. Numerous gravestones made of rough sandstone remind visitors of the courtyard's earlier function as a cemetery. The small church was built at the beginning of the 14th century as a chapel, later expanded in 1440. For centuries, the Lords Kress von Kressenstein served as benefactors to the church. Located in the church's interior are several gravestones and memorial plaques belonging to the family. Further works of art include the Altar of St. Leonhard (1476), the Madonna of Nuremberg (1485) and the altar dedicated to St. Georg, commissioned in 1480. The altar depicts Georg's battle with a dragon. The saints of Nuremberg's main parish churches, Laurentius and Sebaldus, accompany him on the altar's painted wings.

The fortified church, which survived both wars with the margraves unscathed, was set on fire in the night of February 26, 1943 after being hit by a bomb. Reconstruction was completed in 1952, paid for by Samuel and Rush Kress of New York.

Right: Weathered gravestones made of rough sandstone in the idyllic courtyard of the fortified Church of St. Georg in Kraftshof.

Its location, I say, seems not only to be in the middle of Germany, but in the heart of all of Europe. For it lies equidistantly to the Adriatic and Baltic Seas, determining Europe's latitudinal scope. From here it is also the same distance to the Don River as it is to Cadiz, with which Europe's length is measured.
Johannes Cochlaeus, 1512

CITY
IN THE MIDDLE
OF EUROPE

City in the middle of Europe

Pages 78-79: Nuremberg's panaroma, as viewed from the castle, clearly shows the nucleus of the historic old town, as well as the modern buildings and the greenery which surround the city.

The wealth of Nuremberg's citizens is not only renowned in Germany, but as far away as in Spain and in Lisbon, and is famed among the most remote Scythians on the Don River, as well as among the Polish, the Hungarians, indeed in all of Europe. Where may there exist a hidden corner where its moneys and goods haven't reached? Nuremberg's merchants live in Lisbon, Lyon, Venice, Budapest, Krakow, Vienna, Cologne, Antwerp and in all of the trading centers of Europe, where they extend their wealth to the people by conducting trade with them, keeping them from living in scarceness.
Johannes Cochlaeus, 1512

Transportation hub of Europe – center of logistics

The noise of two-cycle engines announced the *Wende* (the turn of events marking the beginning of the reunification between East and West Germany) in 1989/1990. Eastern Bloc makes of cars coming in from Thuringia and Saxony, but also from Western Bohemia – Pilsen and Prague – rattled to Nuremberg. Thus the revival of a thousand year old trade route to the east began, a route which once led to Nuremberg's ascent.

The division of Germany and Europe after the second World War had brought Nuremberg into geographical seclusion, with all the previous transportation routes being blocked off by barbed wire and concrete walls. The math is simple: Prague is located just 300 kilometers from Nuremberg, and as of 1990 the two cities are connected through an official partnership, whose ties reach back deep into the Middle Ages. The route known as the Golden Way or the Via Carolina was commissioned by Karl IV (1316-1378), King of Bohemia and Holy Roman emperor. It passed through the cities of Sulzbach, Weiden, Neustadt, Bärnau, Tachov and Kladruby on its way to the Vltava River Valley. Salt, textiles, oils, figs, leather, copper, pewter and lead were transported along the trade route, a route which was included in the 1380 *Interieur de Bruges*. This map, which was drawn in the Flemish trade metropolis, listed all trade and pilgrimage routes known at the time.

"Nürnberger Tand geht durch alle Land" (the trinkets of Nuremberg are sold to all lands) – the saying referred not just to trade relations with Bohemia. In the 14th and 15th centuries, trade increased immensely, thanks to tariff privileges which Nuremberg enjoyed as an Imperial City. Preferred trade regions were the Upper and Lower Rhein as well as Flanders. There were also active trade relations with Southern France, Austria and Northern Italy, especially with Venice. Nuremberg's trading companies delivered metal and textile products to all corners of the known world. The Nuremberg merchants' nickname "pepper sacks" was gained through the spice trade. Around 1500, Nuremberg even achieved a monopoly in the saffron trade.

In the environs of the city there are no mentionable natural resources. For this reason, the city owed its growing wealth to its central location and to the prowess of its merchants. Up until the Thirty Years' War, Nuremberg's merchants refined their system of maintaining long-distance trade relations by commissioning their own couriers.

The end of the Thirty Years' War marked the end of an era of cosmopolitan openness, and the city lost its prominent status in the empire and in Europe. Many of the problems were self-inflicted: Nuremberg rigidly maintained its medieval social and trade systems into the modern age. At least some craftsmen active in the trades of making musical instruments and mirrors as well as wire-drawers were able to uphold the good reputation of products made in Nuremberg.

Not until the Imperial City was annexed into Bavaria in 1806 did a revival of its distant trade routes begin, accompanied by the Industrial Revolution. One example is the export of gold thread, a cheaper variety of leaf gold. The brass factory at the Hammer Plant, located on Nuremberg's east side, produced this shimmering gold foil which measured only 0.02 millimeters thick, and was popular for adorning temples and mosques in Asia and on the Arabian Peninsula. In the Kingdom of Bavaria, Nuremberg became increasingly significant as a hub of trade: hops, pencils and toys became synonymous with the city's name.

It quickly became evident that all this wholesale activity would require better transportation routes. The Ludwig-Danube-Main Canal, planned as a project of the century, was not as successful as originally hoped. Charlemagne had already had the idea around the year 800 to connect the Rhine and Main Rivers to the Danube. Beginning in 1836, Ludwig I commissioned the construction of the 172 kilometer-long canal between Dietfurt and Bamberg. A harbor was even built in Nuremberg, located on *Rothenburgstraße.* Transportation on the canal, which was under 16 meters wide

A towboat on the Old Canal: Segments of the water route have survived in Gartenstadt and further southeast toward Neumarkt.

City in the middle of Europe

At the time being there are two locomotives in operation in England, each with 20 horsepower, conducted by an English engineer. They are powered by steam only in the afternoons, in the mornings and in the evenings the wagons are pulled by horses.
Friedrich Mayer, 1842

and 1.5 meters deep, joined by around 100 locks and dams, proved to be quite difficult.

At the same time, the railway was catching on: in 1835, the English engineer William Wilson led the first German train from Nuremberg to its neighbor-city Fürth. This invention eventually replaced both the horse-drawn carriages and the horse-drawn barges along the Ludwig Canal. Within three decades, Nuremberg became the most significant railway hub within a radius of a thousand kilometers. Local companies supplied tracks, railcars and locomotives. The city's railroad age lasted over a hundred years, up until the time when the system of highways for automobile traffic was expanded. On the international railway grid, Nuremberg still profits

from its central location and is also connected to the German Railway's net of express trains.

The significance of the railway for the city is still evident today: Already in 1847, the Royal Railway Authority commissioned the construction of a central railway station in Neo-Gothic style, located at the square of today's station. By the turn of the century, the original station was no longer adequate. It was torn down, making way for a Neo-Baroque Railway Palace, completed in 1905. Its Art Nouveau interior served as an entrance to the system of tracks.

Located just a few hundred meters from the Central Station at *Kohlenhof* was the reloading point at the freight depot, built in 1876. It quickly

Page 82: The grand railway station – this neo-baroque building has graced Nuremberg since 1905.

Below: At the crossroads of international railroad transport. Nuremberg's railroad yard is significant to the entire region and beyond.

City in the middle of Europe

outgrew its capacity. Thus plans were drawn for a new railroad yard, which went into operation in 1903. This gigantic system of tracks takes advantage of the incline between Nuremberg's Südstadt and Langwasser. Demonstrating how significantly the railway changed Nuremberg is the *Ringbahn,* a railway which, beginning in 1910, circumnavigated the city, but has since been decommissioned in many of its segments. It spurred development, attracting many companies to the outskirts of the city.

Improvements in public transportation were also necessary within the city. The history of Nuremberg's streetcars began with a horse-drawn train between the Main Station and Plärrer square in 1881 (the German word for trolley or streetcar – *Straßenbahn* – wouldn't be given that name until 1883). Remarkable is the fact that even back then, the neighboring cities of Nuremberg and Fürth organized a joint system of public transportation. From then on, the race was on to extend the inner-city railway system and to develop new urban housing and industrial zones. First with buses, then finally with the construction of a commuter railway system beginning in 1978, the regional transportation system has been able to keep pace with Nuremberg's expansion and the influx of commuters coming in from the region. Nuremberg's regional transportation authority is now Germany's third largest.

Already at the beginning of the 20th century, there were plans to build underground transportation routes. A tunnel under the castle hill, according to a city council vote from the year 1911, was to connect the old town to its northern neigborhoods. However, economic woes and World War II got in the way of these plans. Not until 1965 did construction begin on an underground railway. And once again Nuremberg is charting the course for transportation in the 21st century: Germany's first fully-automated subway is being developed here.

Even in Nuremberg, the city of the railroad, the good system of expressways and highways in the region has replaced the train as the choice means of transportation. 1,100 kilometers of roads are available to motorists within the city limits. City planners have also taken cyclists into consideration, as evidenced by the continuously growing network of bike paths, such as the route connecting the east side of the city to Fürth in the west, following the Pegnitz River.

100 years after the expansion of the railroad, Nuremberg achieved a central position within the network of expressways, the *Autobahn*. Plans were drawn already in the 1920s to build a European network of express highways. The first segments were built as early as 1924, such as the route from Milan to Lake Como. The Nazis began pushing ahead with plans to build the Autobahn in 1934. In Nuremberg as elsewhere, they were able to take advantage of detailed plans which had been drawn up by previous engineers. By 1938, the route Berlin-Nuremberg-Munich-Salzburg had been completed.

November 26, 1964 is the day when the Autobahn from Nuremberg to Würzburg opened, joining it with the industrial regions located to the west. Additional expressways in all directions would later follow. The result of this modern network of expressways is reminisce of historic trade routes: the city is centrally located along the expressway axes Paris-Prague, London-Brussels-Vienna, Stockholm-Zurich-Milan and Berlin-Rome.

This central position makes Nuremberg attractive to logistics operations. Also significant is its combined network of expressways, canals, railways and a high-capacity international airport. In 1972, the Main-Danube Canal, which had been in planning since 1921, was opened to ship traffic between Nuremberg and Bamberg. The project, mocked by critics as "Europe's largest swimming pool", measures 55 meters wide and four meters deep. The projected annual freight volume was originally 18 million tons, but only added up to about seven million tons in its initial years. Since 1992 the canal has also been linked to the Danube at Kehlheim, and is used for the transportation of freight as well as for tourism. Nuremberg's harbor, with its shipping center, is among the best-developed transhipment points in Germany. Covering an area of nearly 350 hectares, the harbor is now home to hundreds of companies.

More and more new companies are also settling near the highly attractive airport, which opened in 1955. International air traffic continues to

Pages 86 and 87: Nuremberg's International Airport located in the north of the city has grown tremendously in recent years. Its sphere of influence extends beyond northern Bavaria to Thuringia, Saxony and to western Bohemia. Several companies have settled in the vicinity, and hotels and parking areas built around the airport have helped make it a vibrant area of Nuremberg.

City in the middle of Europe

City in the middle of Europe

Below and page 89: Nuremberg's Convention and Exhibition Center has developed into a world-renowned meeting place.

increase through airline, charter and freight service. The airport's sphere of influence extends well into northern Bavaria, Thuringia, Saxony and western Bohemia.

Thanks to its infrastructure, the city has developed into a popular convention and trade fair center. The main event – the International Toy Fair –

takes place annually in February. In addition, many other trade fairs have established themselves in Nuremberg. Reminding us of the innovativeness of Nuremberg's citizens throughout its history is the annual inventors' fair featuring the newest in geek technology. Nuremberg is among Europe's top ten convention and trade fair cities.

Half the town became the Pegnitz River/ a provisional bridge was built there hither/ who e'er wished to cross/ had to fear great loss/ ... that the flood ne'er more shall wax, wishes his Nuremberg Hans Sachs.
Hans Sachs 1507

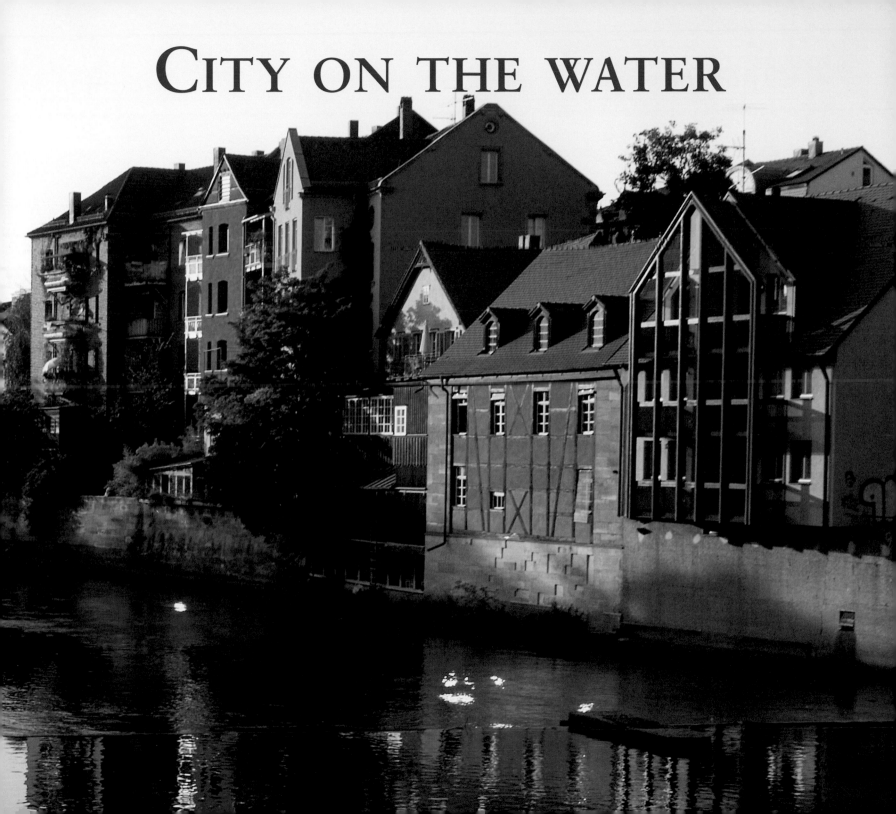

CITY ON THE WATER

City on the water

Pages 90-91: Downstream from the district of St. Johannis, the larger mill Großweidenmühle *once stood at the north bank of the river, while the smaller mill* Kleinweidenmühle *stood on the south bank.*

Below:
The Weinstadel *(Wine Barn) and* Wasserturm *(Water Tower) are among the most picturesque motifs on the banks of the Pegnitz.*

Page 93 top: The rows of homes at Großweidenmühle *display contrasting architecture on the river's edge.*

Page 93 bottom: Located in what is today a restaurant at Großweidenmühle, *the former millworks are still intact.*

On the river lie very many workshops/ Flour mills/ Paper mills/ Copper mallets/ Made there are swords/ shields/ helmets/ knives/ kettles/ all kinds of instruments are forged, as well as all kinds of wires which are drawn from metal.
Janssonius, 1658

In the year 1390, Senator Ulmann Stromer built a magnificently large paper mill near the city with 18 beaters. Elsewhere in Germany it is difficult finding older, more reliable sources pertaining to the development of paper making.
Neues Taschenbuch von Nürnberg, 1822

The Pegnitz

Nuremberg is inseparable from its little river: the Pegnitz was its laundry basin, its garbage dump and the source of power for its craftsmen and later for the city's industrialization. It cut the city in half and kept its citizens watchful because of its devastating floods. Nuremberg's history is closely connected with taming the river which tended to flow too slowly in the summer, but could become a raging torrent within hours of a snow melt or a thunderstorm.

Swampland once surrounded Nuremberg to the east and west along the banks of the Pegnitz. The area on which the Main Market Square was built originally was a swamp which separated the Lorenz and Sebald portions of the old town. Not until the banks of the Pegnitz were drained were Nurem-

---

berg's citizens able to utilize and develop the area. The foundations of these river homes stand on oak posts which – like in Venice – must always be submerged in order not to rot.

Furthermore they possess a river, the Pegnesus, or, according to Sylvius, the Pegnitz, which flows right through the city; it has twelve bridges, six of stone and six of wooden posts, connecting its districts, allowing two islands to form within the city, strewn along the river outside and within the city walls are many mill wheels. It has some millwheels for making flour, others for processing ore, others for making paper, furthermore there are screeching saws which cut tall tree trunks into boards, and there are mills to sharpen knives, and metal workshops. The little river isn't navigable, except for fishermen, but so profitable for the city that it can hardly be overstated.

Johann Cochläus, 1512

Mills

Trough channels, transition ducts and weirs: each generation devised its own techniques to harvest hydropower for mills. Around 1600, there were more than a dozen millworks with an average of three water wheels each along the Pegnitz, including the outlying regions which would later become part of Nuremberg. In addition to the flour mills there were also mills for the production of leather and textiles, sawmills, pulverizing mills and paper mills.

The river achieved tremendous significance as an engine for metal processing: hammering, sharpening, polishing, wiredrawing. Iron ore was mined from the neighboring *Oberpfalz* (Upper Palatinate), known as the "Ruhr district of the Middle Ages". From blank metal, Nuremberg's craftsmen

City on the water

produced weapons, musical instruments and tools. The reformist Martin Luther, for example, was a passionate turner, and ordered his carving tools from Nuremberg.

Bridges

Ford, footbridge, bridge: at the ford at what is today Mögeldorf, several distant pathways met here already before the year 1050. Footbridges were the first attempts to master the Pegnitz's capriciousness, built to allow for a dry-footed river crossing. Bridges finally allowed for the development of a city connecting the Sebald and Lorenz districts, boasting of the metropolis' wealth. The oldest stone bridge in Nuremberg was the triple-vaulted *Maxbrücke*, completed in 1457 and completely renovated in the mid-19th century. It is named for King Maximilian I of Bavaria.

Among the oldest river crossings in the old town are also the *Fleischbrücke* (Meat Bridge) and *Museumsbrücke* (Museum Bridge). The *Fleischbrücke* is considered to be a master architectural achievement, because it spans the water with a single vault. It was built where a double-vaulted bridge dating from 1487 had stood, which was destroyed by the spring flood of 1595. Previously, this ford had also been the site of successive wooden bridges, which connected the city's two districts. A fire and a flood destroyed the original two constructions. In 1595, the City Council aimed to find a permanent solution. Their paragon was the recently completed Rialto Bridge in Venice. Nuremberg's bridge, however, was to be used for transportation, so it was built less steep and incorporated the embankment more than the architects of the Venetian model had. 2,123 oak posts, placed at an angle into the riverbed, still serve today as the foundation of the bridge. The construction even survived the bombs of World War II.

While returning to our quarters we crossed a stone bridge, which is considered here to be a marvel. It has only a single arch, like the Rialto Bridge in Venice, is however neither as high nor as long, rather just about fifty steps across at its furthest distance, over the narrow Pegnitz River. On one

Because the river Pegnitz flows eastward under many arched bridges into the city/ two islands form/ one is overcrowded/ the other convenient for washing/ and hanging up laundry to dry in the sun: this is where the warm baths also are.
After the river has flowed under the twelve bridges, exiting the city/ it moistens the common meeting place/ at which Nuremberg's youth/ as did the Spartans before them on the Eurota River/ convene on holidays to practice such honorable activities/ as archery/ hurling/ wrestling/ jumping/ etc. enjoying themselves.
Janssonius, 1658

end is the Fleischbank [meat bank], over the entrance of which the butchers have installed a ridiculous statue. It is a monstrous, reclining ox, with gilded horns and hooves ... under which this double-verse is engraved in golden letters: OMNIA HABENT ORTUS SUAQUE IN CREMENTA SED ECCE QUEM CERNIS NUNQUAM BOS FUIT HIC VITULUS: MDCXCV

That is: Everything has its origins and descent; but the ox which you see here has never been a calf.

Blainville, 1765

Left: The ox, which had "never been a calf" – this work of art adorns the Fleischbrücke (Meat Bridge).

Page 96: The chancels of the Museumsbrücke (Museum Bridge) bear the inscriptions of Emperor Leopold I and King Joseph I.

Page 97: Where the Pegnitz exits the old town – view of the Kettensteg from the west through the city fortifications.

Pages 98-99: The Triton (fountain of the god of the sea) at the Konrad Adenauer Bridge: A horse with a fish's tail and fins spews water into the Wöhrder See. The bronze statue replicates the Neptunbrunnen (Fountain of Neptune).

Located next to the bridge is the former imperial meat house. A stone ox atop the portal tells of the building's former function as a slaughterhouse and meat shop.

Another historically significant crossing point of the Pegnitz River is located just a few steps to the east. The *Museumsbrücke* achieved its

City on the water

modern appearance in 1954, when it was doubled in width to accommodate increasing automobile traffic. Only delivery vehicles are allowed over the bridge today, thanks to its location in the old town's pedestrian zone. The double-vaulted stone bridge with its characteristic baroque pulpit dates back to the year 1700. The decorative plaques honor Emperor Leopold I and his son, King Joseph I. The name *Josephsbrücke* never took hold, however. The bridge owes its name to the *Gesellschaft Museum* (Society Museum), which began convening in 1809 in the adjacent Franciscan monastery.

Other bridges preceding the *Museumsbrücke* are proven to date back to the 15th century. Located directly under the bridge is the entrance to a flood channel, which drains water out of the Pegnitz during times of flooding.

In the west of the old town, directly at the city walls, stands a monument to technical achievement. In 1824, the *Kettensteg* was constructed as Germany's first suspension bridge. Just one post located in the middle of the river supported the bridge, designed by the master "Mechanikus" Johann Georg Kuppler. In 1930, iron and wooden beams were added to stabilize the bridge. Since then, the bridge no longer vibrates as strongly when crossing.

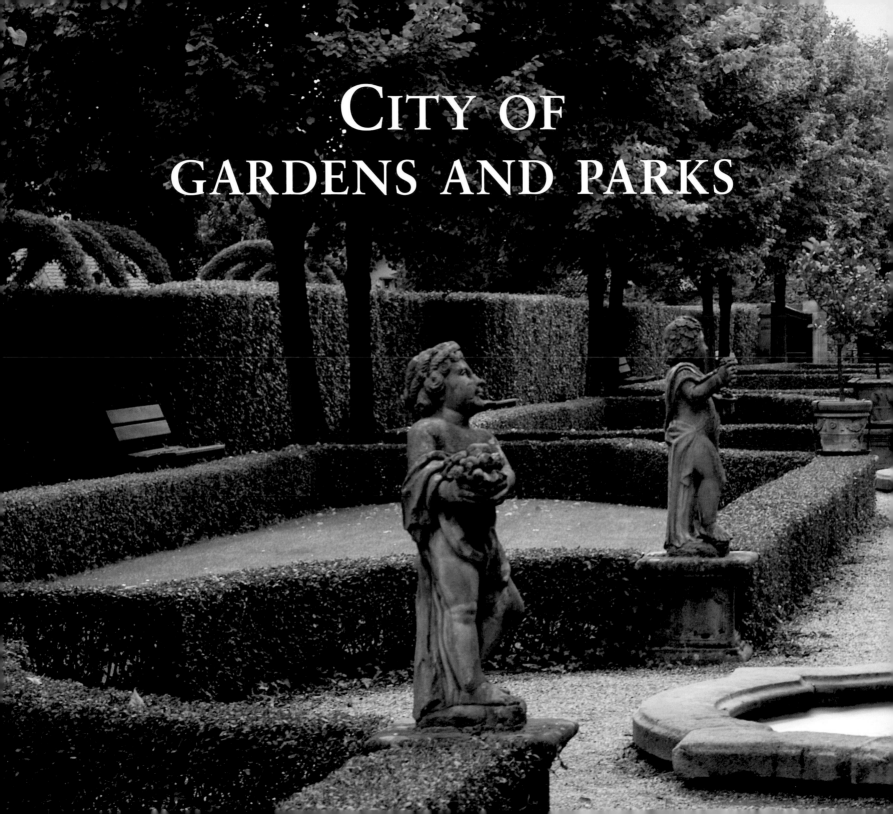

CITY OF
GARDENS AND PARKS

City of gardens and parks

Pages 100-101: The Four Seasons *was the name given to the meter-high putti located in the baroque gardens in the St. Johannis district (Johannisstraße), sculpted of sandstone by an unknown artist at the beginning of the 18th century.*

The history of the Reichswald *(Imperial Forest) is closely tied to the city's own history. The wood of the forest, which at one time mainly consisted of oak, was used to build and fuel the city. Because of continuous plundering of the forest by city residents, the Nuremberg councilman Peter Stromer (or Stromeir) in 1368 began systematically planting coniferous trees in Lichtenhof, marking the begin of planned forestry in Europe: for the first time, wood was not only cut down and cleared, it was systematically planted as a renewable resource. Still today the Reichswald extends into the city limits and, measuring 23,000 hectares, is among the largest contiguous forests in Germany. Large farm fields characterize the city's landscape structure to the north, with* Knoblauchsland *(Garlic Country) serving as Nuremberg's vegetable garden. On an area covering 800 hectares, farmers in the Nuremberg, Fürth and Erlangen tri-city region produce vegetables which are sold at Nuremberg's Main Market Square and throughout the area.*

Page 103: Even in the densely-populated old town, here high above the Henkersteg, shade trees thrive.

Gardens

More than 300 gardens, some over 10,000 square meters in size, surrounded the city fortifications already by the end of the Middle Ages. The patricians and the citizenry of Nuremberg maintained the gardens, which included herbs which had been brought back from the Mediterranean by merchants. Sought-after fruits of the Orient, such as figs, lemons and oranges, were also grown. A 1708 copperplate book on botany authored by Johann Christoph Volkamer, who maintained trade relations with Italy and the Arabic world, detailed the characteristics of the citrus and bitter orange family of plants and the art of growing them in Nuremberg (*"Nürnbergische hesperides oder gründliche Beschreibung der edlen Citronat- / Citronen- und Pomerantzen-Früchte"*). The harsh winters in Nuremberg made year-round, outdoor cultivation of these plants impossible, therefore a system of potted plants and greenhouses was devised.

In the Baroque period, the city's gardening culture was refined at the *Hesperidengärten* (Hesperian Gardens). Most of these gardens, which many used to raise their own supplies of food, were sacrificed during the city's residential and industrial expansion. But some have survived, especially in the district of St. Johannis, where partitioned gardens in the French style can still be admired.

Parks

Unused land within the city walls was rare due to the city's dense urbanization. Due to this situation, the City Council purchased a meadow in St. Johannis outside the walls in 1434, and named it for its previous owner, Berthold Haller. The *Hallerwiese* offered a shady retreat thanks to its numerous basswood trees, just a few steps outside the city walls. Thus Nuremberg had its first public park, which soon became a venue for sporting events and festivals. Archers made use of the facilities, and even executions were carried out on the meadow. By the mid 19th century, three more parks were laid out: the *Rosenaupark* at Plärrer, the *Kolleggarten*, including Platner's Park in the Nordstadt, as well as the *Kühberg* at *Tier-*

City of gardens and parks

gärtnertor on the north side of the castle hill, which provides an excellent opportunity for fast sledding in winter.

The city's industries not only devoured huge swaths of land, they also were responsible for creating Nuremberg's *Stadtpark* (City Park). In 1882, the first "Bavarian state industrial, commercial and art exposition" was held at *Maxfeld*. A state commission aimed to promote the economic advancements made by famous citizens of Nuremberg such as Friedrich

Klett and Sigmund Schuckert, but also those made by the pencil-making dynasties Schwanhäuser, Staedtler, Faber and Lyra. Smaller companies were also given the chance to display their products on the twelve-hectare grounds.

Franz Elpel, who would later become Nuremberg's parks director, acted as an assistant architect planning the new grounds: pavilions and other indoor facilities were built throughout the huge park. The expo attracted two million visitors, and at night they could enjoy the facilities which were lit by electric lamps provided by the Schuckert company. Nuremberg didn't only experience tremendous improvements because of the electricity which the expo brought it – the people also didn't want to do without their new park. Citizens fought to preserve the grounds after the expo, and Elpel installed a rose garden in the park, which would soon become one of the most beautiful of its kind in Germany.

The grounds of *Luitpoldhain* also served in 1906 as a venue for an arts, crafts and commercial exposition. Three times larger than the *Stadtpark*, it was named for the Bavarian Prince Regent Luitpold. Franz Elpel was once again was put in charge of planning the grounds.

Another traditional recreational area is the green zone surrounding *Dutzendteich*

Among the popular places of amusement for Nuremberg's inhabitants is the so-called Dutzend-Teich. There, at this pond of considerable size, is located a public house, which is surrounded on all sides by forest. The pond received its name Dutzend-Teich because in this area are located around twelve other smaller ponds, some of which have been recently turned back into meadows. This recreational area is located half an hour to the east of Frauenthor. In the summer one can ride in gondolas and rowboats; in winter many amuse themselves on the frozen pond, riding sleds or skating.
Johann Ferdinand Roth, 1813

(Dozen Ponds). In 1495 the Free Imperial City Council purchased this man-made lake, and beginning in the 16th century it was a popular destination in Nuremberg for recreational outings. Ice skating in the winter, rowing – later sailing as well – in the summer. In 1911, the city also established public swimming facilities here.

After 1933, the surface area of the lake was dramatically reduced to make room for the Nazi Party Rally Grounds. Today, *Luitpoldhain* and *Dutzend-teich,* including the fair grounds, comprise a large recreational area located on Nuremberg's southeast side.

The 120 hectare area known as *Marienberg* was once the site of Nuremberg's airport, and is now a popular park. The area in the north of Nuremberg, bordering on *Knoblauchsland* (Garlic Country) has traditionally served as a recreational area. The Tucher Brewery once maintained several ponds there, which provided ice for their icehouses located throughout the city. The largest of these ponds served in summer as a swimming hole. The area which today comprises Marienberg Park was the site of Nuremberg's first airport from 1933 to 1943, which in 1955 was relocated a few kilometers to the west, bordering a large forest. After 1945, the grounds of what would later become Marienberg park served as a dump for the rubble from the war-damaged Nordstadt. In 1959, construction began on the spacious park grounds.

Gartenstadt

Fighting poverty, providing housing in the greenbelt, living with a sense of community: these were the objectives of England's Garden City Movement which reached Germany in the late 19th century. In Nuremberg there are several examples of greenbelt urban planning, helping to alleviate the acute housing shortage during the age of industrialization. Often tenants had the right (or obligation) to keep small farm animals and to plant vegetables, fruit and berries for their own use. In 1908, 255 founding members signed the charter which formed the housing cooperative Gartenstadt. In 1911, the first moved into their homes built on inexpensive land located to the south of the city. Richard Riemerschmied, an architect from Munich, designed the new settlement.

Similar projects with large gardens and green zones were developed in Werderau and near the *Rangierbahnhof* (railroad yard). In Altenfurt, settlers there in the 1920s attempted to breed silkworms. The business idea folded just after a few years because of cheaper imports from Asia.

Zoo

The cultural landscape of the southern slope of the *Schmausenbuck*, located in eastern Nuremberg, has been home to the city zoo since 1939. Where sandstone had once been chiselled out of the hill, now exotic animals found new abode in the pits and caves of the former quarries. Nuremberg's people

Lions have found a new dwelling place in a former sandstone quarry.

City of gardens and parks

have from the very beginning had a special relationship with their zoo. Beginning in the mid 19th century, other cities had long since established zoos. In Nuremberg, the project was long overdue: several residents applied for shares in the new zoo corporation.

The original zoo opened in 1912 and was located on *Bayernstraße* (Bavaria Street) near *Dutzendteich*. Only because of the generosity of the city's citizens was it possible to keep the animals from starving during World War I and during the following years of economic turbulence.

In 1936, a new home had to be found for the animals to make room for the Nazi Party Rally Grounds, which were to be built on the grounds at *Dutzendteich* according to plans by Albert Speer. Next to all of the buildings located at *Schmausenbuck* fell victim to war bombs in August of 1943. After the end of the war, freed forced laborers who had sought refuge in the forests surrounding Nuremberg slaughtered around 300 of the zoo's animals.

But the bond which Nuremberg's citizens had with their zoo, even after the end of the war, was not to be broken. Twelve days after the end of the war, the 63 hectare area reopened its gates. Reconstruction on the facilities was completed after twelve years. Expansion would later follow, including construction of the Dolphinarium.

The fondness which city residents have had for their zoo was not only evidenced in the years after the war, when families would go on a Sunday pilgrimage travelling by streetcar. Every elementary school class would also visit the zoo at least once per year. Therefore it is of no surprise that private initiatives have played an important role in zoo expansion. Apart from the gifts of generous donors, a fundraising club comprised of "friends of the zoo" has taken on many important responsibilities.

Today, the zoo is considered to be a major tourist attraction in North Bavaria. With its international breeding and exchange programs, the municipal zoo has also achieved scientific recognition as a research institution.

Pelicans aren't the only birds with an affinity to the ponds at the zoo – many wild aquatic birds also flock here.

CITY OF
FOUNTAINS

City of fountains

City of fountains

A register from 1810 lists 137 public fountains, almost as many as the number today, nearly 200 years later. However, Nuremberg's residents at the beginning of the 19th century relied on these fountains as their source of clean drinking water. But even then, most of the bubbling works of art weren't designed for every day needs – for buckets and washtubs – but to serve as eye-pleasers.

Hanselbrunnen

The oldest fountain in the city is considered to be the *Hanselbrunnen* in courtyard of the *Heilg-Geist-Spital*. The sculpted depiction of the musician's wait-pipe, onto which the water flows, dates back to the year 1389. For security reasons, a replica was placed in the fountain in 1913. The original "Hansel" can be viewed at the Germanic National Museum.

Schöner Brunnen

The famed *Schöner Brunnen* (Beautiful Fountain) located on the Market Square is also a replica. The sandstone of the original, which was crafted by Heinrich Behaim from 1385 to 1396, had heavily eroded. Around the year 1835, Nuremberg commissioned a replica. Between 1897 and 1902, the porous sandstone was replaced with shell limestone. During restoration, the rung platform was given an additional annulus. The heavily eroded sandstone figures were brought to the Germanic National Museum, three statues of heads of the prophets were taken to the State Museums in Berlin.

The first plans for the construction of the octagonal work of art date back to the time of Emperor Karl IV and the year 1370, on the occasion of the square's revamping. After the pogroms against the Jews in 1349, in which 562 people were killed, the city confiscated the former Jewish quarter located on the grounds which would later comprise the main market and fruit market, demolishing all existing buildings in the process.

The tower of *Schöner Brunnen*, measuring 19 meters high, looks like a painted Gothic church tower. Its four levels of sculptures depict the medie-

It isn't easy finding a city in Germany so richly endowed with running water, with pipes and fountains, as Nuremberg. Even taking Augsburg into consideration: Nuremberg's man-made water system is older. Flowing to a number of fountains and drinking water basins, water is channelled from far away, for example to the market square's Schöner Brunnen, to the so-called Hainzenbrunnen in the hospital courtyard, and to the drinking water basins on Insel Schütt. In some cases, the well water comes from above, powered by water wheels in the Pegnitz or Fischbach rivers by mechanically pushing the water onward; for example toward the fountain at town hall, in the new addition, and to St. Lorenz. It reaches the latter by way of a 60 foot high tower, which is near the city gates at Frauenthor, part of the city fortifications, which had already been generated by the turbines in the Fischbach River, which are well worth seeing. Every hour at least 100 buckets of water are pushed four storeys high into two large basins – many deep wells of stone are located in the depths of the moats, which are all inter-connected. The water is driven upward, with the help of six barrels attached to three cross beams and a triple metal crank, all set in motion by a water wheel which the Fischbach faithfully powers.
Christian Gottlieb Müller, 1793

Pages 110-111: The fountain known as the Schnepperschützenbrunnen, created in 1904 by Leonhard Herzog, conjures up the image of the crossbowman to visitors of the meadows of the Haller-wiese. In Nuremberg's oldest park, these men known as Schnepperer first arched their bows in honor of Emperor Friedrich III in 1487.

Left: Double Gothic: Schöner Brunnen *(Beautiful Fountain) and the* Frauen-kirche *(Church of Our Lady) on the Main Market Square.*

The fountain is aptly named "beautiful fountain", for it rises in an ancient fashion like a pyramid, higher than 60 feet upwards, made completely of stone, level for level, youthful, light and blithe, so delicately adorned with statues of prince-electors, kings, heroes from Jewish, Roman and German history, not even Moses and the prophets have been omitted, till it all finally comes to a climax with two fantastic flowers on top, and a weather vane at the very peak.
Gottfried Wilhelm Becker, 1836

City of fountains

val world view: philosophy and the seven liberal arts form the first level, placed above them are the four evangelists with the four Latin Fathers of the Church, the third row is reserved for the seven prince-electors and the nine great heroes, including David, Alexander the Great, Caesar, King Arthur and Charlemagne. Placed above them are Moses and the seven prophets. The uppermost level, located below a helmet decorated with crabs, has no statues.

According to legend, he who turns the golden ring placed in the decorative latticework on the southeast side of the fountain will one day return to Nuremberg. Another tradition says that if you turn the ring you are granted one wish. An apprentice is said to have installed the ring, on which no seam can be seen, in order to impress his master.

Gänsemännleinbrunnen

Just a few steps from *Schöner Brunnen*, located in the courtyard of the town hall, is the *Gänsemännleinbrunnen* (Little Goose Man Fountain), molded of bronze by Pankraz Labenwolf in 1550. True to nature, the figure depicts a farmer dressed in traditional 16th century garments, carrying two geese under his arms to the market. The inventory of the *Fembohaus* includes a model of the goose farmer, carved out of basswood.

Ehekarussel (Hans Sachs Fountain)

The realism of Labenwolf's *Gänsemännlein* was the basis for another Nuremberg fountain, built 430 years later: the *Ehekarussel* (Marriage Carousel), located on *Ludwigsplatz* (Ludwig Square) in front of the *Weißer Turm* (White Tower). The 14 meter wide carousel, designed by the artist Jürgen Weber of Braunschweig (Brunswick) depicts one of Hans Sachs' poems. The shoemaker and poet had dedicated the poem "The Bittersweet Marital Life" to his wife. The *Meistersinger* Sachs is himself depicted, dancing atop the cusp of the fountain. Statues made of painted bronze and marble have, since the fountain's construction in 1984, depicted the crude, drastic and sometimes romantic aspects of marriage.

Page 114, left: In the town hall courtyard stands Pankraz Labenworf's fountain, known as the Gänsemännleinbrunnen. *The sculpture is a product of German Renaissance folk art.*

Page 114, right: mythical creatures dominate the Ehekarusell (Marriage Carousel), *in front of the* Weißer Turm (White Tower).

Everywhere I see around me
rise the wondrous world of Art:
fontains wrought with richest sculpture
standing in the common mart.

And above cathedral doorways
saints an bishops carved in stone,
By a former age commissioned
as apostles to our own.
Henry Wadsworth Longfellow, ca. 1880

City of fountains

The vile excuse for commissioning the work was to disguise a subway shaft. Otto Peter Görl, the city's long-serving architectural advisor, staunchly supported the construction of the work of art, which was initially highly controversial because of its "plumply sensuous" depictions.

Neptunbrunnen

Outside the old town, located in Nuremberg's City Park, is the *Neptunbrunnen* (Fountain of Neptune). Many chapters of Nuremberg's city history are contained in this work of art, a testament to the joys of lavish baroque composition. The fountain was built between 1660 and 1669 according to plans by the sculptor **Georg Schweigger** (1613-1690) and the goldsmith **Christoph Ritter** (1610-1676). The statues were molded in the atelier of **Wolf Hieronymus Herold** (1627-1693). Originally, this stylish baroque art was intended to replace the *Schöner Brunnen* on the Main Market Square. Instead, the stones for the fountain base remained for nearly 200 years outside the city fortifications, near *Frauentorgraben*. Just briefly, around the year 1700, was the fountain temporarily put on display.

In 1797, when Nuremberg was facing an enormous burden of debt, Tsar Paul I made the Free Imperial City an offer. He bought the fountain and had it placed in the gardens of the Peterhof Palace near St. Petersburg. Almost 100 years later, Nuremberg remembered its fountain and had a plaster molding made of the original. In 1901, a Jewish hop trader, Ludwig Ritter von Gerngros, financed a replica of the fountain, which was placed on the Main Market Square in 1902. In 1934, the Nazis had the work of art removed because it was supposedly in the way of their military parades, and moved it to a new site on *Marienplatz*. In 1962, the Fountain of Neptune stood in the way of the construction of a new bus terminal, and it was again moved to City Park. On several occasions, plans were made to move the fountain onto the square between the churches of St. Jakob and St. Elisabeth. While the underground was being built, preparations were even made for the fountain's installation. But the project fell through because of its costliness, and the Fountain of Neptune is still located in City Park.

In the city of Nuremberg proper there are a hundred and twenty-eight main streets, and four hundred small streets, twelve large fountains and a hundred and thirty-three smaller fountains, a hundred and seventeen drinking fountains, sixteen churches, forty-four sacred buildings, twelve bridges, ten market places, three hundred and sixty-five towers belonging to the city fortifications, twenty thousand homes, seventy-five public houses, and it requires three hours to circumvent it and its suburbs ...
Johann Georg Keyßler, 1751

The original fountain returned to Nuremberg in 1942 as looted art during the war. It survived the war in an art bunker and was returned in 1947 to its St. Petersburg location.

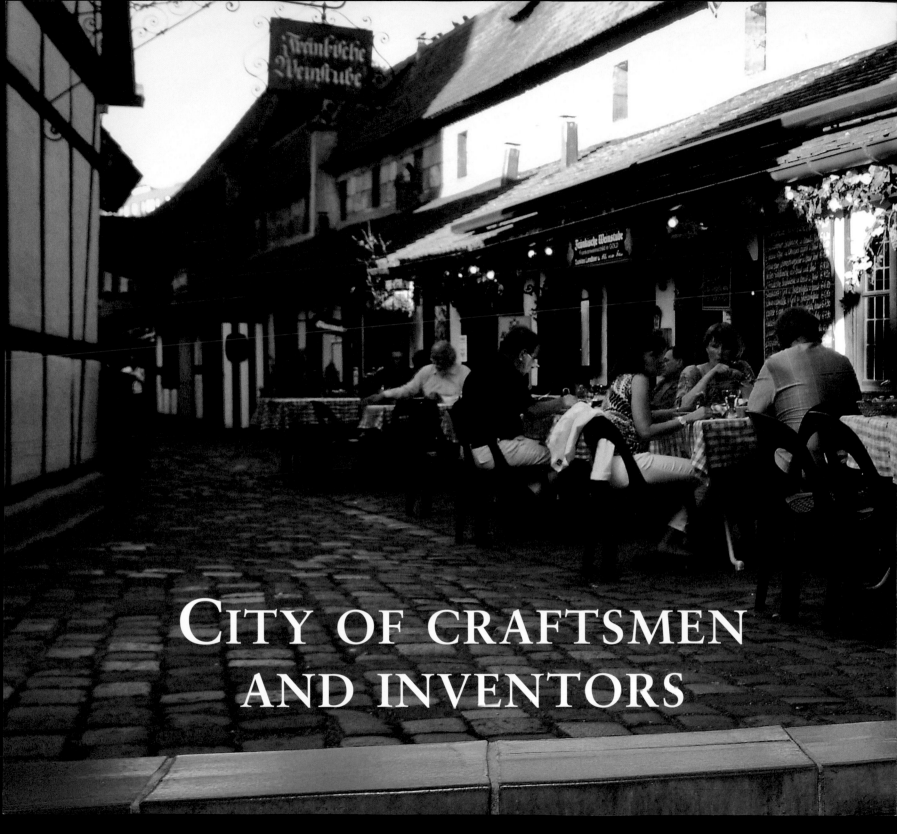

CITY OF CRAFTSMEN AND INVENTORS

City of craftsmen and inventors

Gingerbread, clarinets, pocket watches and paper tissues: these are just four of an endless list of products which originated in Nuremberg. Before 1806 however, the city hadn't always thrived under an atmosphere of innovativeness. The Council repeatedly forbade new production methods. But the proverbial craftsmen's cleverness prevailed against authority. Several of the inventions were simple devices, such as the thimble, screw clamp and jaw vise, which quickly became indispensable. Other inventions included the fire hose and a special kind of wheel chair.

Gingerbread production developed here already in the Middle Ages as a result of the flourishing spice trade. Nuremberg cannot claim exclusive rights to the bratwurst, which is a spicy meat mixture encased in sheep's intestines. The European Commission voted to protect the "Nürnberger Bratwürste" label in 2003. And the word "Tempo" – dubbed by the United Paperworks in Nuremberg – has since 1929 been synonymous in German-speaking countries with the word for paper handkerchief.

He is considered to be the inventor of the pocket watch, and at the very least he contributed significantly to the fine mechanics of the watch: **Peter Henlein** (ca. 1485-1542) reduced around 1510 the size of mainsprings which were used on locks, triggering through the implementation of feather brakes a steady, slow release of energy. His watches required neither a pendulum to regulate the precision of its cycles, nor weights to keep it in motion. Later generations referred to these sought-after, precise time indicators as *Nürnberger Eier* (Nuremberg Eggs). The term however didn't refer to their shape, it was a distortion of the Latin word "hora", or hour.

In lieu of a system of patent protection, Nuremberg's guild of craftsmen protected their inventions by limiting access to certain trade secrets. Members of these guilds were only allowed to carry out their trade within the city. Under no circumstances were they allowed to reveal trade secrets while out of town. Such restraints were also placed on wiredrawers, a trade which was considered to have originated in Nuremberg. As early as the 14th century, masters and their apprentices were drawing the hot metal through perforated plates. The trade reached its peak through advancements during the 16th century, for example in the production of violin strings and spectacle frames.

Toys were always part of the product offering. The first dolls, called *Nürnberger Docken* were first made of ceramic and later of various materials. Beginning in the 17th century, pewter figurines made in Nuremberg were popular among children.

Armor made in Nuremberg was also in demand over many centuries. Suits of armor and coats of mail made in the city on the Pegnitz offered soldiers improved range of motion. Beginning in the 16th century, customers came to purchase firearms of all kinds.

Augustin Kotzer was the name of the inventor who in 1630 developed a barrel with twisted rifling, controlling a projectile's trajectory.

Science also profited from Nuremberg's precision metal-shaping. The *Zirkelschmiedsgasse*, a street in Nuremberg's old town, is named for the compass makers who once worked there. The astronomer and mathematician, **Johannes Regiomontanus** (1436-1476) – actually, his last name was Müller, but selected a Latin translation of his hometown Königsberg – was attracted to Nuremberg because of the good reputation of the precision metal workers in the

Suits of armor were popular articles of export out of the city-state on the Pegnitz.

City of craftsmen and inventors

City of craftsmen and inventors

Page 122: Several streets' names pay tribute to the tradition of craftsmanship in Nuremberg. This is a picture of the Weißgerbergasse, a street where tawers (leather workers, similar to tanners) were once active.

Page 123: Romantic courtyard in the Weißgerbergasse.

Page 125: "Father Schuckert": The innovative entrepreneur Johann Sigmund Schuckert took the well-being of his employees to heart.

A main product of Nuremberg origin is gold and silver lace-work. 3,000 people live from this trade alone in the city. Local compass makers also produce scale pans, gold balances, brooches, mathematical fixes and much more. A large amount of the beaten gold is exported to England, and demand is often so high that some orders must be turned down. Spectacles, tins, buttons, pencils and such are made in large numbers in the homes of the people, and everybody, including women and children, participates in their production. Tins are sold at a price of a dozen for twelve Kreutzer; pencils at a price of one gilder for twenty-four dozen. The reason why so much work gets done here is primarily because of the contentedness of the people.
Jonas Ludwig von Hess, 1798

city. His pupil **Martin Behaim** (1459-1507) created the 1492 globe which is considered to be the oldest surviving depiction of the earth as a sphere. Depicting the known world of the day – not including the 1492 discovery of America – the globe is a masterpiece of Nuremberg's craftsmanship.

Jakob Bulmann deserves mentioning here for his gigantic model of the rotating solar system (ca. 1520).

Hardly recognized are the accomplishments of the inventor **Georg Hartmann** (1489-1564). As a scientist, he applied his knowledge to watch making and discovered the inclination of the compass' centerpin.

Also contributing to the fame of Nuremberg's artisan craftsmanship was the **Schwanhardt** family, a dynasty of glass cutters dating back to the 17th century. They developed new techniques in etching.

The spirit of discovery evident among Nuremberg's artisan craftsmen lives on with the legacy of the all-round mechanical genius **Hans Lobsinger** (1519-1584), whose interests included instrument making, chemistry, pyrotechnics and whose thoughts inspired other curiosities. For example, **Hans Hautsch** (1595-1670) attempted to build an elevator, a wheelchair for gout patients and a "self-driver": already in 1649, he had dreamed of inventing an automobile.

The tradition of musical instrument making in Nuremberg goes back to the city's earliest days. However, it wasn't its trumpets, trombones or horns which would later enter music history encyclopedias, rather a single woodwind instrument: the invention of the clarinet is attributed to **Johann Christoph Denner** (1655-1707). He attached two additional keys onto the shawm, increasing the instrument's range upwards.

In the 19th century it was the industrialists who received attention for their new products. The miller's son **Johann Wilhelm Späth** (1786-1854) replaced wooden millwheels with an iron construction and developed, among many other machines, a mechanical digger to remove earth for the Ludwig-Danube-Main Canal.

The pencil-making tradition in Nuremberg goes back to the 16th century. Already at the beginning of the 17th century, writing utensils were a popular export. But there was also outside competition in the business. In France, a graphite compound was developed which provided stronger, more durable lead, and became the industry standard by the mid 19th century. 23 writing utensil manufacturers were located in Nuremberg and vicinity in 1900. Brand names such as Faber-Castell, Lyra, Schwan-Stabilo and Staedtler represent this manufacturing tradition.

One of the men responsible for making the Siemens Company name famous throughout the world is a Nuremberg native: **Johann Sigmund Schuckert** (1846-1895). He impressed his contemporaries in 1874 by devising a gigantic generator, powered by the Pegnitz River. Schuckert had spent years travelling the world, learning his trade, taking him to Siemens & Halske in Berlin and to the Thomas A. Edison laboratory in the United States. First with arc lamps, then with Edison's light bulbs, Nuremberg received new nocturnal lighting. He was also a pioneer in developing spotlights, and later streetcars.

After his death, his factory merged with Siemens. He earned the nickname "Father Schuckert" for the way he took care of his employees in a socially responsible manner.

CITY OF MUSEUMS

City of museums

Pages 126-127: Past and present in dialogue – the medieval city fortifications are reflected in the glass façade of the Neues Museum (New Museum).

Right: Kohlrabi and culture – Schloss Neunhof (Neunhof Palace) is home to a subsidiary of the Germanisches National-museum *(Germanic National Museum).*

Nuremberg is full of beautiful and strange things, and already in the Germanic National Museum I walked myself silly for two hours. But I wouldn't want to live in this city, I find it too crowded between the sky-high buildings with their tall, pitched roofs.
Jakob Burckhardt, 1877

Precious collections

The patrician-bourgeois awareness of their responsibility to maintain cultural treasures for later generations dates back to the time of Albrecht Dürer. Already during his lifetime, Nuremberg stored a considerable number of paintings in its town hall, which by the 18th century included 300 precious works of art. Private patrician collections and a huge number of libraries added to the value of the city's collections. Among the private holdings, the collection of 24,000 books belonging to the universally educated natural scientist Christoph Trew is considered to be the most valuable of these treasures.

Stadtbibliothek

Since 1429 there has been a city library in Nuremberg, the oldest in Germany. Among its holdings are not only books, but also curiosities and various manuscripts. The City Library evolved out of the *Ratsbibliothek* (Library of the City Council), which carefully maintained its writings since the 14th century. Later it attested to the excellent standing which Nuremberg had as a city of book printing.

Address: Stadtbibliothek Nürnberg, Egidienplatz 23
www.stadtbibliothek.nuernberg.de

Germanisches Nationalmuseum

The founding of the Germanic National Museum dates back to a tribute made by the German Federal Convention in 1853 to Nuremberg in honor of its historical significance in the Middle Ages. The Franconian nobleman, Hans von Aufseß, pushed hard for this initiative, which aimed to preserve – against the trend toward sectionalism – national treasures: history, art and literature.

Initially housed in the tower at *Tiergärtnertor*, the museum was moved in 1857 to its current location, the former Carthusian order monastery. The former church, two cloisters, three monks' dormitories and the refectory comprise the focal point of the collection. Several additions have increased the museum's size to 50,000 square meters. 1.2 million objects, dating from pre-historic times up to modern art are housed in this gigantic treasure chamber. The museum's holdings include the former international art collection of the *Gewerbemuseum* (Industrial Arts Museum), which was a separate museum until 1988, as well as a collection of historic musical instruments and medical and pharmaceutical equipment.

Schloss Neunhof (Neunhof Palace; Neunhofer Schlossplatz 12), is a subsidiary of the Germanic National Museum, and is also worth visiting.

Germanisches Nationalmuseum, Kartäusergasse 1; Management, Library, Graphic Arts Collection, Coin Collection and Archives: Kornmarkt 1.
www.gnm.de

DB-Museum and Museum für Kommunikation
Nuremberg has been the home of a museum of transportation since 1899, opened as the *Königlich Bayerisches Eisenbahnmuseum* (Royal Bavarian Railway Museum). In 1902 it received a separate postal museum department. The collections, which consist both of originals and of models, attest to the history of the railroad in Germany since the *Adler's* first trip in

City of museums

1835. In addition, the history of the development of the postal system, including the telephone, is displayed here. Philatelic enthusiasts can view a collection of approximately 200,000 stamps.

DB-Museum and Museum für Kommunikation, Lessingstraße 6

Stadtmuseum Fembohaus
On display in this building, the largest surviving private home in Nuremberg's Old Town, is a 1930s carved model of the medieval city which was destroyed by the bombs of World War II. Covering five floors, the museum documents essential aspects of city history, including an historic kitchen, a review of the history of music in Nuremberg, and imposing interiors featuring oil paintings and elaborate stucco.

Stadtmuseum Fembohaus, Burgstraße 15

Albrecht-Dürer-Haus
In 1509, Albrecht Dürer purchased this residence on the square known as *Tiergärtnertorplatz,* in which he dwelled until his death in 1528. The home served as his living quarters, atelier and as the place where he carried out his theoretical studies. In 1826, the city bought the home. At the end of the 19th century it was furnished with period furniture. Today, with its low ceilings, the home gives an impression of what it was like to work and live in Dürer's day. Also helping to make history come alive are scenes played by actors in the kitchen, or a reconstructed printing press.

Albrecht-Dürer-Haus, Albrecht-Dürer-Straße 39

Tucherschloss and Hirsvogelsaal

This 1544 palace commissioned by Lorenz Tucher is a testament to Patrician culture. After being destroyed in 1945 by fire bombs, it was rebuilt in the late 1960s. This garden and summer residence, located directly in the city, demonstrates the period of transition from the Middle Ages to the Renaissance and harbors precious features, such as altars, faiences and oil paintings.

The adjacent Hirsvogel Hall built in the year 1534 with its interior design is considered to be a Renaissance masterpiece. Peter Flötner carved the allegories of farming, hunting, craftsmanship, measurement, music and war. The ceiling fresco titled "The Downfall of Phaeton" is comprised of 20 canvases, painted by Georg Pencz, a student of Dürer's.

Tucherschloss and Hirsvogelsaal
Hirschelgasse 9-11

Spielzeugmuseum

In the Dürer commemorative year of 1971, the city's toy museum was opened in a former merchant's home. The objects on exhibit attest to the links between Nuremberg's merchants and the places of production in Thuringia, Saxony's mountainous region *Erzgebirge* and in the Alps. Also impressive are the collections of tin toys made in Nuremberg's production facilities.

Spielzeugmuseum, Karlstraße 13-15

Left: The Stadtmuseum *(City Museum) located in the* Fembohaus *(Fembo House) attests to the wealth of Nuremberg's citizens and displays objects of importance to the city's history.*

Above: The Tucherschloss *(Tucher Palace) and the* Hirsvogelsaal *(Hirsvogel Hall) reward visitors with masterpieces of interior design.*

City of museums

Neues Museum

The New Museum is impressive on account of its bold architecture: Volker Staab of Berlin drew the plans for the first Bavarian state museum outside Munich. The building, which opened in 2000, incorporates a city collection which Nuremberg had been compiling since the 1960s, along with exhibits from the *Neue Sammlung* (New Collection) from the State Museum for Applied Arts in Munich. The design department concerns itself with objects of daily use, including a VW Beetle, chairs and eating utensils. Richard Lindner, Joseph Beuys, Georg Baselitz, Tadeusz Kantor – these are just a few of the names of artists represented here. Special exhibitions and events are also held here on a regular basis.

Neues Museum, Staatliches Museum für Kunst und Design, Klarissenplatz, Luitpoldstraße 5
www.nmn.de

Dokumentationszentrum Reichsparteitagsgelände

Already the architecture of the Documentation Center distances itself from the conjoined *Kongresshalle,* the monumental Nazi construction. The architect Günther Domenig of Graz, Austria, has hurled his steel entrance into the original main building like a spear. Consciously attached to the building as a foreign body, the study rooms hover above the uncompleted building.

Since opening in 2001, the museum's centerpiece has been the exhibition "Fascination and Violence". Altogether, 18 rooms document the tyranny of the National Socialist regime, from their beginnings to their party rallies, anti-Semitic policy and racial purity laws, up until the Nuremberg Trials. The history and usage of the surrounding grounds since 1945 is also explained.

Dokumentationszentrum Reichsparteitagsgelände, Bayernstraße 110
www.dokumentationszentrum-nuernberg.de

> I can tell you, that in this company for the first time I truly came to appreciate wonderful Nuremberg, with its art treasures and bridges and gardens and tree-lined avenues and beautiful fountains ... The wealth of Nuremberg's art treasures is still considerable. They have begun restoring the old paintings and buildings in the spirit of their own period.
> *August von Platen, 1821*

Schwurgerichtssaal 600

Here in the east tract of the Nuremberg *Justizgebäude* (Palace of Justice), the trials of the International Military Tribunal took place in 1945 and 1946. At the main trial, 24 major war criminals were accused of instigating a war of aggression and of genocide. Until 1949, Courtroom 600 was the venue for twelve follow-up trials.

Schwurgerichtssaal 600, im Justizgebäude, Fürther Straße 110

The Justizgebäude *(Palace of Justice), located on* Fürther Straße, *was the scene of the famed Nuremberg Trials.*

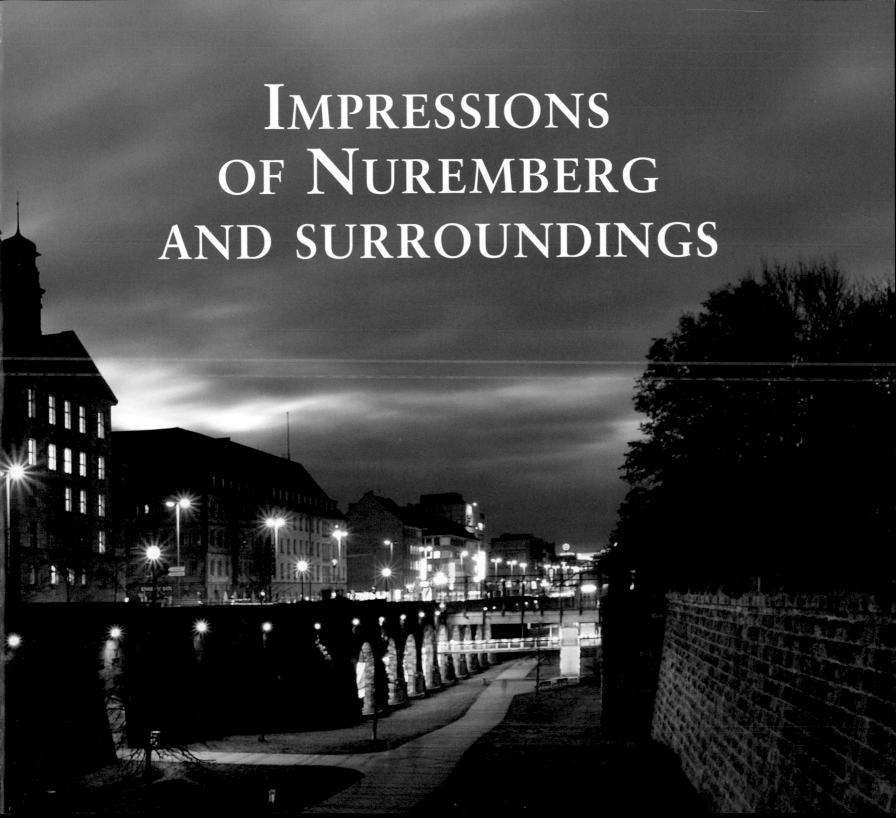

IMPRESSIONS
OF NUREMBERG
AND SURROUNDINGS

Pages 134-135: Today's State Opera opened in 1905 as a municipal theater, located just outside the city walls. The opera house's architecture was heavily influenced by the art nouveau style.

Left: Impressive mansions built by wealthy citizens, such as this one located on Pirckheimer Street, are imaginatively adorned, in keeping with Nuremberg's particular variation on the art nouveau style.

Page 138: Evening light in Knoblauchsland *(Garlic Country). This agricultural area located to the north of Nuremberg provides the city with fresh vegetables.*

Page 139 upper left: Glass greenhouses with sophisticated climate regulation facilitate vegetable growing in "Little Holland", as Knoblauchsland *is sometimes called.*

Page 139 bottom left: A city surrounded by forests – here a view from the castle toward the east, looking onto the range of hills known as Schmausenbuck.

Page 139 right: The headquarters of the insurance company Nürnberger Versicherung *tower over the nearby forest, the Sebalder Reichswald.*

Pages 140-141: Concerts such as "Classic in the Park" at Luitpoldhain *attract thousands of visitors every year.*

Impressions of Nuremberg and surroundings

The Author

Lorenz Bombard, M.A., was born in Nuremberg in 1961. While still attending high school he received musical training at the Meistersinger Conservatory in Nuremberg. Beginning in 1980 he studied History, German, Political Science and Sociology at the Universities of Marburg, Munich and Erlangen. Following his studies he worked as an educator, dramaturge, journalist, translator and copywriter; since 1989 he has been on the editorial staff of the *Nürnberger Nachrichten* newspaper.

The Photographer

Rainer Elpel, also a Nuremberg native, was born in 1951 and is a free-lance photographer taking on advertising and commercial assignments as well as working for renowned magazines, publishing houses and calendar printers. Previously released illustrated books: Franconia, Scotland and New Zealand. The photographer has also achieved renown through expressive and insightful audio-visual projects. In 1992 he co-founded Travel Media, an agency for audiovisual media. His photographic journeys have taken him all across Europe, to the Caribbean and to New Zealand.

Cover: The castle towers above the city. Still today it is the focal point of Nuremberg, which half a million people call home.

Back cover, upper left: The Hauptmarkt *(Main Market Square) with its* Schöner Brunnen *(Beautiful Fountain).*

Back cover, upper right: Sculpture at the Hesperidengärten *(Hesperian Gardens).*

Back cover, bottom left: A dancer performing in the historic town hall – Nuremberg is also artistically a city of contrasts.

Back cover, bottom right: Historic buildings are reflected in the glass façade of the Neues Museum *(New Museum).*